It's another Quality Book from CGP

This book has been carefully written for children working towards a Level 3.

It matches the Attainment Targets perfectly.

There's lots of stuff to learn if you want to get a Level 3. Happily this CGP book explains all the important information as clearly and simply as possible.

It's also got some daft bits in to try and make the whole experience at least vaguely entertaining for you.

What CGP is all about

Our sole aim here at CGP is to produce the highest quality books — carefully written, immaculately presented and dangerously close to being funny.

Then we work our socks off to get them out to you — at the cheapest possible prices.

Contents

Section Four — Understanding Shape

Section Five — Measuring

Section Six — Handling Data

Section Seven — Using and Applying Mathematics

Published by CGP

Editors:
Charlotte Burrows, Katherine Craig, Charley Darbishire, Sarah Hilton, Sharon Keeley, Rob MacDonald, Andy Park, Michael Southorn, Luke von Kotze, Julie Wakeling, Sarah Williams.

Key Stage Two Consultant:
John Cullen

ISBN: 978 1 84762 194 8

With thanks to Paul Jordin, Ali Palin, Rachel Selway and Lucy Towle for the proofreading.
With thanks to Jan Greenway for the copyright research.

Thumb illustration used throughout the book © iStockphoto.com.

Groovy website: www.cgpbooks.co.uk

Printed by Elanders Ltd, Newcastle upon Tyne.
Jolly bits of clipart from CorelDRAW®

Based on the classic CGP style created by Richard Parsons.

About the Book

This Book has All the Tricky Topics for Level 3

You've got a good chance of getting a Level 3 if you can do all the maths in this book.

There are a couple of pages on each topic.
One page explains the maths.
The other page has worked examples.
These show you how to answer questions.

This book covers all the Attainment Targets for Level 3. They say what maths children working at Level 3 can usually do.

There are Practice Questions for Each Section

At the end of each section are practice questions.
You can see what you know and what you don't know.

There's a matching Level 3 Question Book.
It's got questions on all the topics.
It also has some practice tests too.

There are Learning Objectives on All Pages

Learning Objectives say what you need to know.
Use the tick circles to show how well you understand the maths.
Use a pencil. You can tick other circles as you get better.

Tick here if you can do some of the Learning Objective.

If you're struggling, tick here.

Tick this circle if you can do the Learning Objective really well.

Learning Objective:

"I know facts about regular polygons such as the number of sides and number of angles."

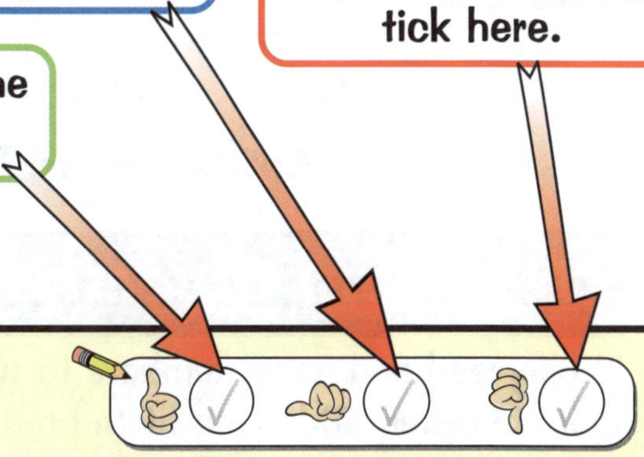

Numbers and Number Lines

Place Value

The value of a digit depends on its place in the number.

The digit on the right is the units.
Then it's the tens.
Then it's the hundreds.
Then the thousands.

Th	H	T	U
		7	6
	3	4	2
1	5	0	0

Two-digit numbers don't have any hundreds so they're smaller than three-digit numbers... which are smaller than four-digit numbers.

Ordering Numbers

EXAMPLE: Put these numbers in order, smallest to biggest: 254, 540, 95, 249.

Look at the hundreds first:

254 540 95 249

540 — This is biggest. It's got more hundreds than 254 or 249.

95 — This is smallest. It's got no hundreds.

So 254 and 249 are in the middle. But which is bigger?

They both have 2 hundreds.

So look at the tens. 254 is bigger than 249.

So the right order is 95, 249, 254, 540.

Number Lines Show the Order of Numbers

Numbers are in order on a number line. This means they get bigger with each step to the right. Number lines go on forever.

4 is to the left of 7 because 4 is a lower number than 7.

EXAMPLE: Draw an arrow to show where 260 would be on this number line.

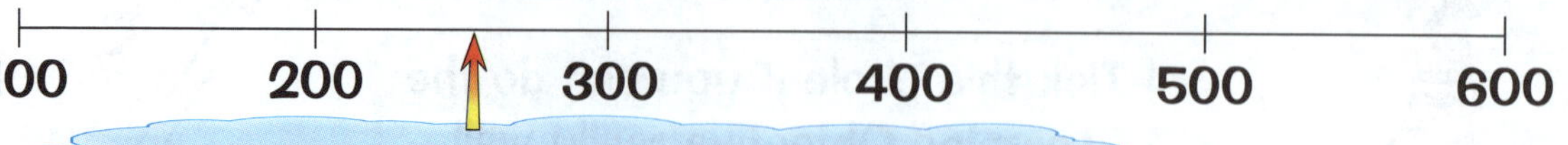

260 is just over halfway between 200 and 300.

Learning Objective:

"I can read and write numbers to 1000. I can put them in order, and place them on a number line."

Numbers and Number Lines

Question 1

Write these numbers in order from smallest to largest: **776 882 97 196 185**

1. First look at the hundreds. You can see that 97 is the smallest as it has no hundreds.

2. 776 and 882 are the largest as they have 7 and 8 hundreds.

3. 196 and 185 both have 1 hundred. Look at the tens. 196 has 9 tens, and 185 has 8 tens, so 196 is larger than 185.

776 882 97 196 185

97 ... ...

97 ... ... 776 882

97 185 196 776 882

So the order is:
97 185 196 776 882

Question 2

Here is part of a number line.
What number is the arrow pointing to?

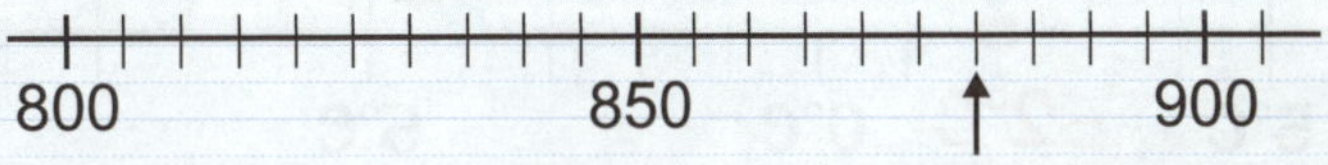

1. The number is more than 800 but less than 900 so the hundreds digits must be 8.

2. Work out what one "jump" on the number line is. From 850 to 900 there are 10 jumps.

3. Start at 850 and count on 5 for every jump.

Between 800 and 900:
The number must be 8_ _

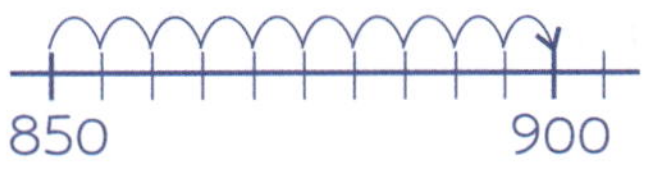

10 jumps = 50, so 1 jump = 5.

Six jumps of 5 along from 850:

= 880

Numbers get bigger as you go up the number line...

It's worth putting in a bit of extra practice with number lines. If you're ever stuck on a number problem it should help to sketch out a number line — they're really, really useful.

Numbers and Number Lines

Negative Numbers are Less than Zero

The number line is really useful for understanding negative numbers.

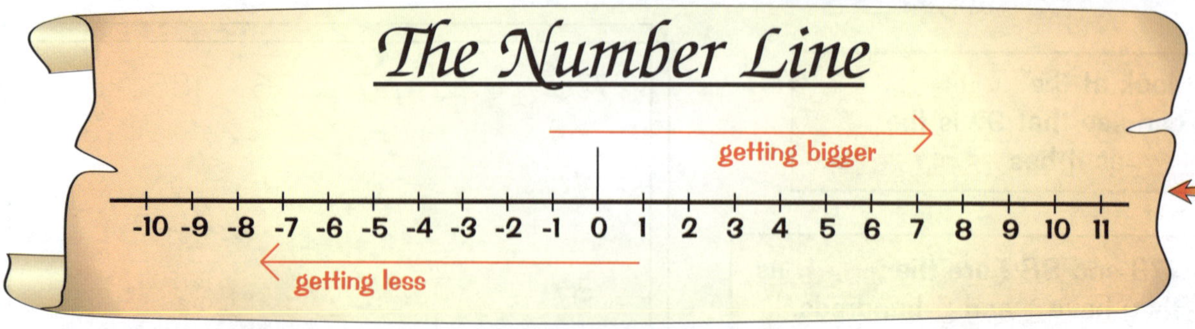

It goes on forever in both directions but that won't fit on the page.

All positive numbers are to the right of zero.
All negative numbers are to the left of zero.

Negative Temperatures are Below Freezing

EXAMPLE: It's 4 °C in Swansea. It's 6 °C colder in Liverpool. What is the temperature in Liverpool?

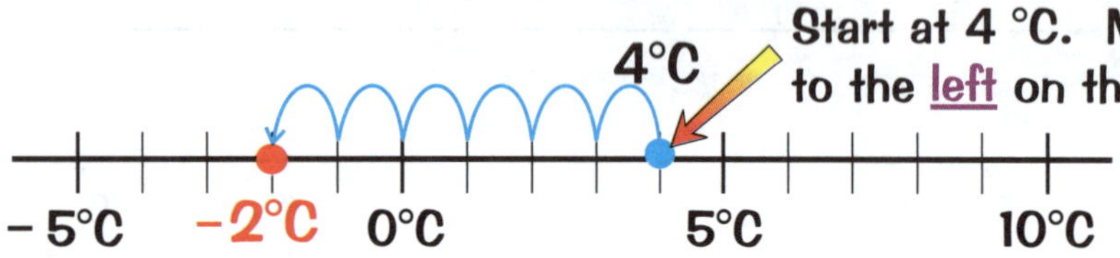

Start at 4 °C. Move 6 places to the left on the number line.

4 – 6 = –2

The temperature in Liverpool is –2 °C.

Use < and > to Compare Numbers

You can use the symbols < and > to show whether one number is bigger or smaller than another.

For example, 5 is greater than 2 so you can write 5 > 2.

< means 'is less than'
> means 'is greater than'

EXAMPLE: Put the correct symbol in each box.

7 ☐ 3 → 7 is greater than 3, so 7 > 3

–5 ☐ –3 → –5 is less than –3, so –5 < –3

It's easy to think that -5 is greater than -3 because 5 is greater than 3. But -5 is less than -3 because it's further to the left on the number line.

Learning Objective:

"I can place positive and negative numbers on a number line and use inequality signs."

Numbers and Number Lines

Question 1

The temperature in Gwen's freezer is –4 °C.
Gwen's fridge is 9 °C warmer than her freezer.
What is the temperature in Gwen's fridge? Show your working.

1. First mark –4 on a number line.
2. Then count on 9 steps.
3. The number you get to is your answer.

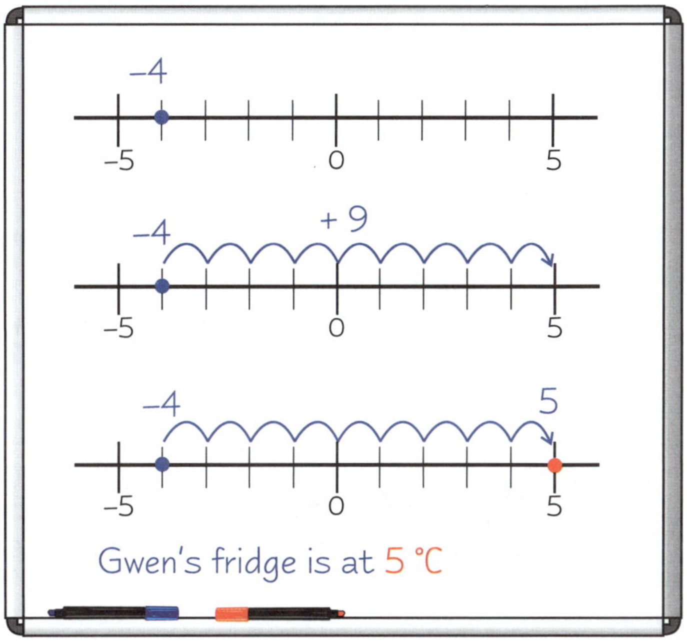

Question 2

Use the symbols < and > to make the following number sentences correct.

a) 2 ☐ 6 b) –1 ☐ –3

a)
1. Draw a number line. Mark on the numbers in the question. 2 is further to the left than 6. So 2 is less than 6.
2. The wider end of the symbol goes next to the greater number.

b)
1. Make another number line. –1 is further to the right than –3. So –1 is greater than –3.
2. So the wider end of the symbol must go next to –1.

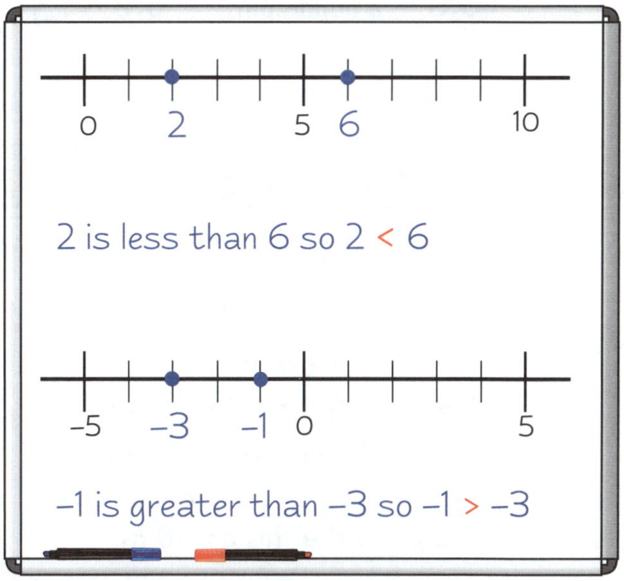

Make sure you get < and > the right way round...

It's easy to get < and > mixed up. But here's a way to remember them — the wider end of the symbol goes next to the greater number. So for example, 5 > 4, or –3 < 4.

Decimals

Decimals Have Tenths and Hundredths

Decimals are one way to write numbers that aren't whole numbers.
The digits to the right of the decimal point are all worth less than 1.

Tens Units Tenths Hundredths

16.37

Decimal point

18.1 is just a bit bigger than 18.
18.9 is just a bit less than 19.
18.5 is right in the middle between 18 and 19.

You can partition decimals. Partitioning means breaking down into parts.

For example...
7.82 can be partitioned into 7 + 0.8 + 0.02

7 units, 8 tenths and 2 hundredths.

You Can Show Decimals on a Number Line

You can use a number line to show where decimals are.

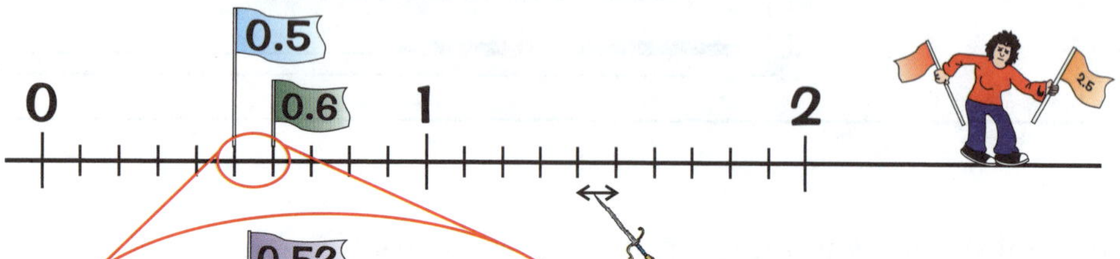

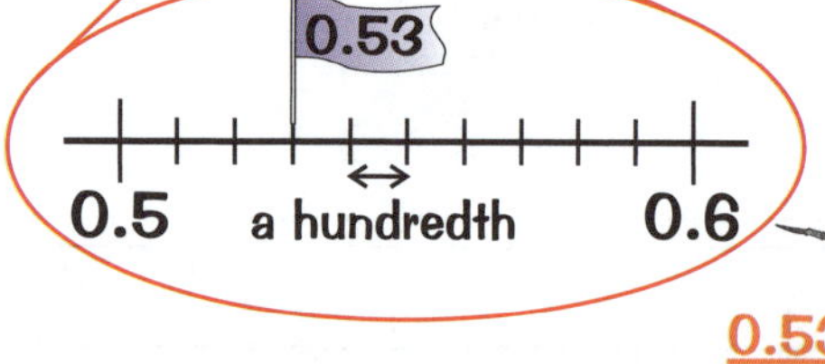

Each unit on the number line is split into ten of these parts. So each of these little parts is a tenth.

One tenth can then be split into ten hundredths.
0.53 is 5 tenth parts and 3 hundredth parts to the right of zero.

Decimals are Used in Money and Measuring

Decimals are used in measuring.
Centimetres are hundredths of a metre.

So, 1 m and 7 cm is 1.07 m
1 m and 26 cm is 1.26 m
1 m and 60 cm is 1.60 m

You can write this as 1.6 m.

Decimals are also used in money.
Pence are hundredths of a pound.

So, £1.23 is £1 and 23p
£1.05 is £1 and 5p
£1.50 is £1 and 50p

Money is always written with two decimal places, even if there are just 0s on the end. You write £1.50, not £1.5

Learning Objective:

"I can use and partition decimals with tenths and hundredths. I can place decimals on a number line."

Decimals

Question 1

Partition 23.97 into tens, units, tenths and hundredths.

1. The 2 is in the tens place. So it represents 2 tens.
2. The 3 is in the units place. So there are 3 units.
3. The first digit after the decimal point is the tenths. There are 9 tenths.
4. The second digit after the decimal point is the hundredths. There are 7 hundredths.

T U . t h
23.97 — 2 tens = 20

23.97 — 3 units = 3

23.97 — 9 tenths = 0.9

23.97 — 7 hundredths = 0.07

So 23.97 = 20 + 3 + 0.9 + 0.07

Question 2

Here is part of a number line.
What number is the arrow pointing to?

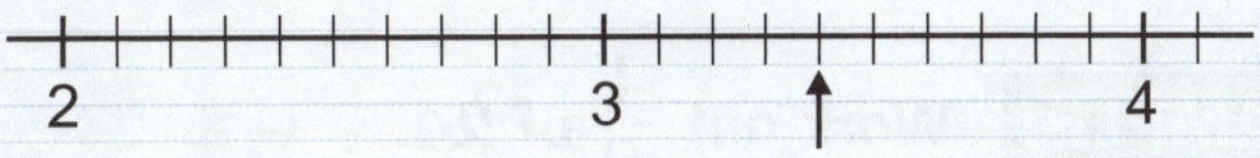

1. The arrow points to a number bigger than 3 but less than 4, so there are 3 whole units.
2. Work out what each division is worth. Count the "jumps" on the line between the numbers.
3. Count the number of tenths from the 3 to the arrow.
4. Put your units and tenths together.

Between 3 and 4:
The number will be 3._

10 jumps between each unit.
So the line is split into tenths.

4 tenths on from last unit:
4 tenths = 0.4

So the arrow points to 3.4

Anything less than a unit goes after the point...

Nearly every time you buy something you use decimals — every penny is one hundredth of a pound. The next time you're in a shop see if you can partition some of the prices.

Using Fractions

Find Fractions of Shapes by Counting

To understand fractions, you need to remember this:

The bottom number of a fraction is called the denominator. It tells you how many equal parts something is split into.

$$\frac{1}{2}$$

The top number is the numerator. It tells you how many of those equal parts you've got. So this fraction is just another way of saying 1 out of 2.

EXAMPLE: What fraction of this triangle is yellow?

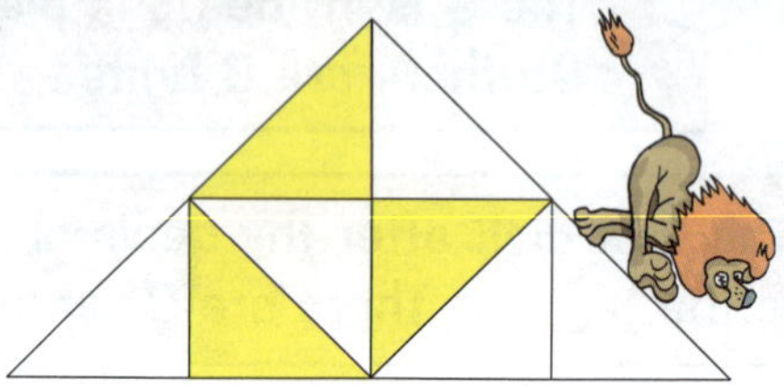

ANSWER: The triangle is split into 8 equal parts. 3 out of the 8 parts are yellow. So the fraction of the triangle that's yellow is $\frac{3}{8}$.

Divide by the Denominator

To find half of something, you divide it by 2. To find a third of something, you divide it by 3. And so on...

...you divide by the denominator... $\frac{1}{5}$

$\frac{1}{5}$ of 15 = 15 ÷ 5 = 3

EXAMPLE: Work out $\frac{1}{6}$ of 24.

ANSWER: Divide by the denominator, which is 6. → 24 ÷ 6 = 4

You could use that answer to work out a harder one, like $\frac{2}{6}$ of something.
$\frac{1}{6}$ of 24 is 4, so $\frac{2}{6}$ of 24 is 2 × 4 = 8.

Equivalent Fractions Have the Same Value

Diagrams can help to show that fractions are equivalent.

For example, $\frac{4}{16}$ is equivalent to one quarter. Here's why...

$\frac{4}{16}$ =

= $\frac{1}{4}$

Learning Objective:

"I can find fractions of a shape or a number.
I can spot when two fractions are equivalent."

Using Fractions

Question 1

Dermot has a bar of chocolate that looks like this: 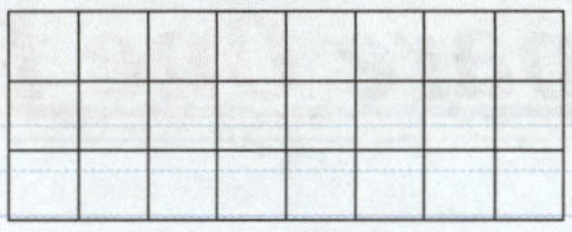

He eats $\frac{1}{4}$ of the chocolate bar. How many small squares of chocolate are left?

1. First work out how many small squares there are in the whole bar.
2. Dermot eats $\frac{1}{4}$ of the 24 squares. You need to divide 24 by 4 to find out how many squares this is.
3. So Dermot eats 6 squares. Now you can work out how many are left. Subtract 6 from 24.

There are 3 rows of 8 squares.
So there are $8 \times 3 = 24$ squares.
(Or you could just count the squares.)

$24 \div 4 = 6$ squares

So $\frac{1}{4}$ of $24 = 6$

$24 - 6 = 18$ squares

Question 2

Which of these shapes have $\frac{2}{3}$ shaded?

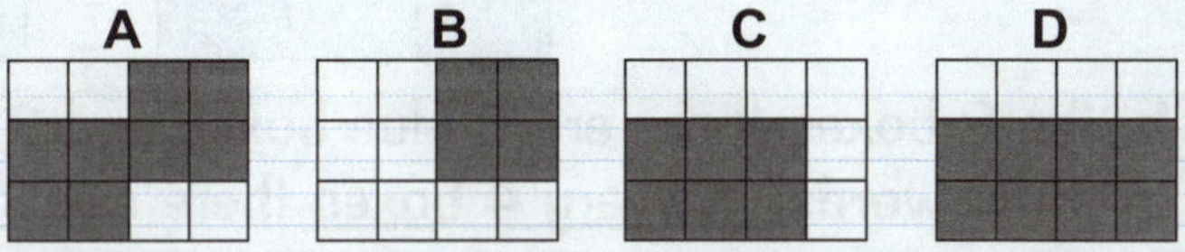

1. Count the total number of small squares in each shape.
2. Find $\frac{1}{3}$ of the 12 small squares. You need to divide 12 by 3.
3. Multiply $\frac{1}{3}$ by 2 to find $\frac{2}{3}$.
4. So $\frac{2}{3}$ means that 8 out of 12 squares will be shaded. Count how many small squares are shaded in each shape.

Each shape has 3 rows of 4 squares.
So each has $3 \times 4 = 12$ small squares.
(Or you could just count the squares.)

$\frac{1}{3}$ of $12 = 12 \div 3 = 4$ small squares

$\frac{2}{3}$ of $12 = 4 \times 2 = 8$ small squares

A and D have 8 squares (or $\frac{2}{3}$ shaded).

B and C have 4 and 6 squares shaded.
(so less than $\frac{2}{3}$).

Sharing things out means you'll get a fraction...

Fractions are pretty much a piece of cake... cut into equal slices. The bottom number is how many slices the cake is cut into, and the top number is how many slices you munch.

Proportion and Ratio

Ratios Compare One Part to Another Part

Look at this pattern:
There are 2 white boxes and 6 red boxes.

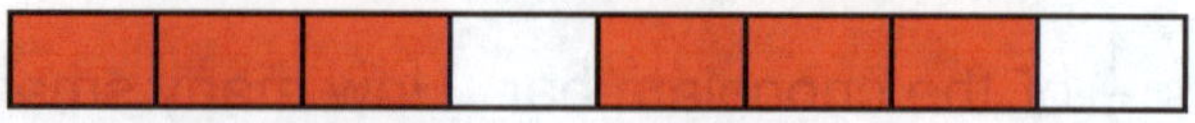

Another way to say this is "For every 1 white box there are 3 red boxes".
You can say that the boxes are 'in the ratio' 1 white to 3 red.

EXAMPLE: For every 5 pizzas Simon buys, he gets 1 free salad.
If he buys 20 pizzas, how many free salads does he get?

ANSWER: The ratio is 5 pizzas to 1 salad.

To get from 5 pizzas to 20 pizzas you multiply by 4.
You need to do the same to the number of salads.

5 pizzas to 1 salad
$\times 4$ $\times 4$
20 pizzas to ? salads

$1 \times 4 = 4$ free salads.

Proportions Compare a Part to the Whole Thing

You can also describe a pattern with proportions.

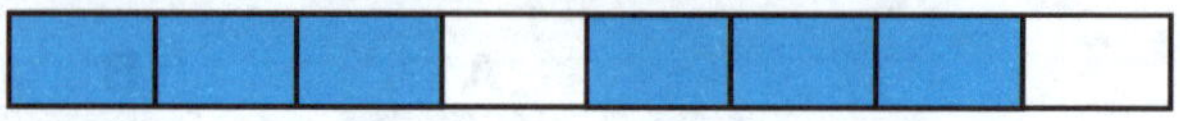

In the 8 boxes there are 6 blue boxes and 2 white boxes.
In other words, in every 4 boxes there are 3 blue boxes and 1 white box.

The proportion of blue boxes is 3 in every 4.
The proportion of white boxes is 1 in every 4.

EXAMPLE: The picture shows Gemma's fish bowl.
What proportion of the fish are pink?

ANSWER: There are 9 fish in total, and 3 of them are pink.
So the proportion of fish that are pink is 3 in every 9.
You can simplify this to 1 in every 3.

Proportions are really another way of writing fractions.
The proportion "1 in every 3" is the same as the fraction $\frac{1}{3}$.

Learning Objective:

"I can solve simple ratio and proportion problems."

Proportion and Ratio

Question 1

Claire makes a scale drawing of a badminton court.
2 cm on her drawing represents 1 m on the real court.
Her drawing is 26 cm long. How long is the real court?

1. For every 2 cm on Claire's drawing there is 1 m on the court. You need to know how many metres there are for 26 cm.

2. So work out how many lots of 2 cm there are in 26 cm.

3. There are 13 lots of 2 cm in 26 cm. So the real court must be 13 lots of 1 m long.

2 cm to 1 m

26 cm to ? m

× 13: 2 cm to 1 m → 26 cm to ? m

1 m × 13 = 13 m

So the real court is 13 m long.

Question 2

Marcus is a fisherman. 1 out of every 4 fish that he catches is a cod.
One day he catches 3 cod. How many fish does he catch that day in total?

1. First write down the proportion of cod.

2. The question says he catches 3 cod. You can draw a diagram to help you find out how many fish are caught altogether.

OR. You could do it another way. Just multiply the number of fish by 3 (because there are 3 times as many cod caught in total).

1 cod in every 4 fish

The shaded fish are cod:

So there are 3 cod in every 12 fish.

× 3: 1 cod in 4 fish. → 3 cod in ? fish.

Total caught = 3 × 4 = 12 fish.

One exam question for you, three pies for me...

Read ratio and proportion questions really carefully. '1 for every 3' means something very different from '1 in every 3'. You might find drawing a diagram helpful too.

Rounding

Rounding Whole Numbers to the Nearest 10...

"Rounding to the nearest 10" means finding the nearest number ending in 0.

- If the last digit is less than 5, round down to the ten below.
- If the last digit is 5 or more, round up to the ten above.

5 is the important number because it's halfway between two tens. For example, 25 is halfway between 20 and 30.

EXAMPLE: Round 34 to the nearest 10.

You can see it on a number line. 34 is less than 35 so 34 rounds down to 30.

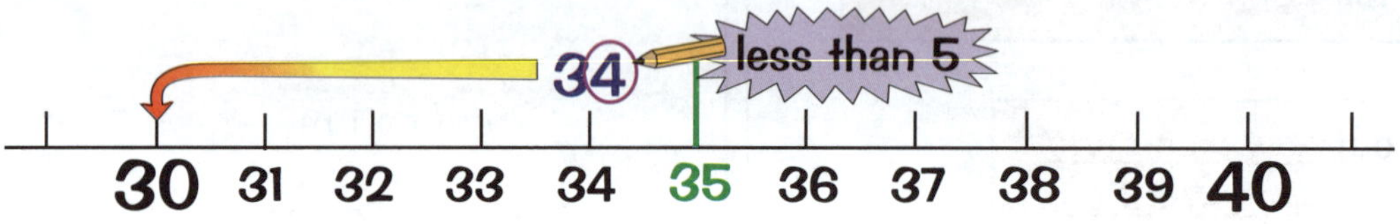

...or the Nearest 100

"Rounding to the nearest 100" means finding the nearest number ending in 00.

- If the last two digits are less than 50, round down to the hundred below.
- If the last two digits are 50 or more, round up to the hundred above.

EXAMPLE: Round 172 to the nearest 100.

172 is between 100 and 200. 72 is more than 50 so 172 rounds up to 200.

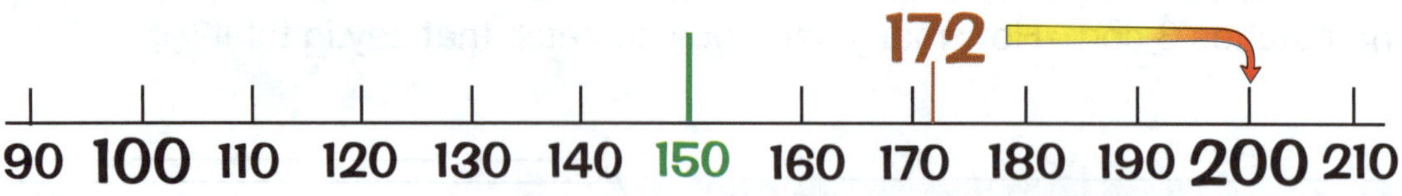

Use Rounding to Estimate Answers

You can estimate the answer to a calculation by using rounded numbers. Rounding numbers makes calculations much easier.

An estimate is a close guess.

EXAMPLE: Estimate the answer to 123 + 29.

1. Round both numbers to the nearest 10.
   123 + 29
   ↓ ↓
   120 + 30

2. Then work out the rounded calculation: 120 + 30 = 150

   So 123 + 29 is about 150.

Learning Objective:

"I can round numbers to the nearest 10 or 100, and I can use rounding to estimate a sum or difference."

Rounding

Question 1

Round **345** to a) the nearest 100 b) the nearest 10

a) 1. Decide which pair of hundreds 345 is between.

2. Decide which hundred it is closest to by looking at the last two digits.

b) 1. Decide which pair of tens 345 is between.

2. Decide which ten it is closest to by looking at the last digit. If it's 5 or more you round up.

345 is between 300 and 400.

The last two digits of 345 are less than 50, so 345 is closer to 300.
345 rounds down to 300.

345 is between 340 and 350.

The last digit of 345 is 5,
so 345 rounds up to 350.

Question 2

Estimate the **difference** between 39 and 181.

1. Write down the calculation that you're estimating the answer to.

2. Round both numbers to the nearest 10. Rounding to the nearest 100 isn't sensible here because the numbers are too small.

3. Now do the calculation using the rounded numbers. The answer is the estimate you need.

181 – 39

39 rounds up to 40

181 rounds down to 180

So 181 – 39 is approximately 180 – 40.
180 – 40 = 140
So the difference between 39 and 181
is approximately 140.

Rounding — just go to the nearest ten (or hundred)...

Estimating is a great way to check that your answer is about right. For example, if your 'proper' answer is 3835 and your estimate is 40, something's gone wrong somewhere.

Practice Questions

1 Write these numbers in order from smallest to largest.

643 227 284 109 84

2 The store room in Emile's restaurant has its temperature set using the dial below. The arrow shows the current temperature.

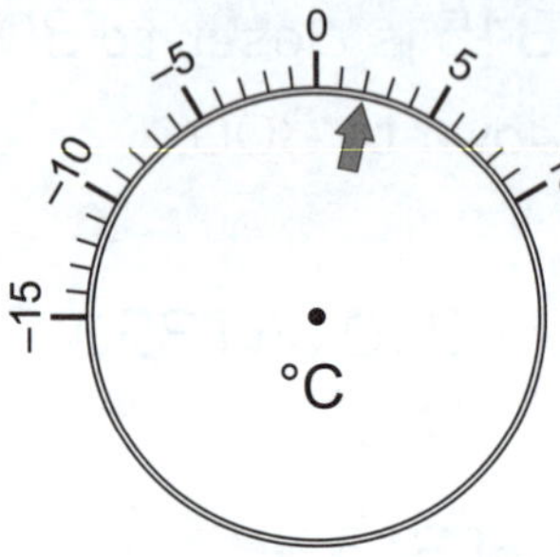

Emile turns the temperature down by 6 °C.
What will the new temperature be?

3 Copy these number sentences. Put either < or > in each box to make them correct.

a) 5 ☐ 1 b) 8.4 ☐ 9.4 c) –8 ☐ 7

4 Partition 13.45 into tens, units, tenths and hundredths.

13.45 = ☐ + ☐ + ☐ + ☐

5 Copy this number line.

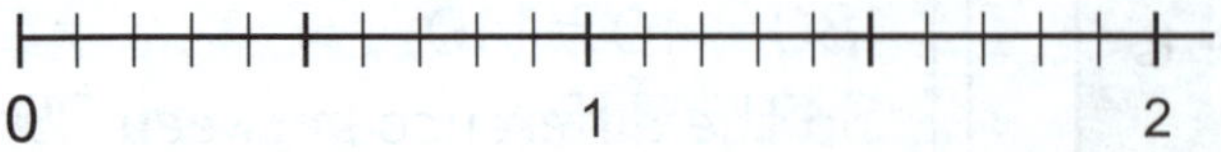

a) Draw and label an arrow pointing to 1.2

b) Draw and label a second arrow pointing to 1.85

Practice Questions

6 Konrad's knitting was 1 metre long. He knits an extra 5 centimetres.

How long is Konrad's knitting now? Give your answer in metres as a decimal.

7 Carlos buys a pie and nine tomatoes.
He eats the pie and tomatoes on Friday, Saturday and Sunday in equal portions.

a) How many tomatoes did Carlos eat on Friday?

b) What fraction of the pie did he eat in total on Friday and Saturday?

8 Look at these shapes.

A 

B 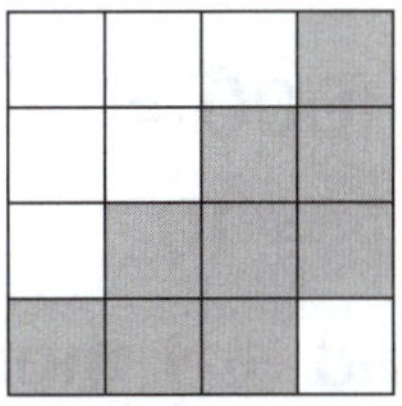

C 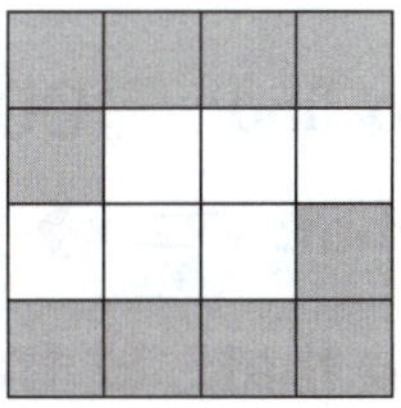

D 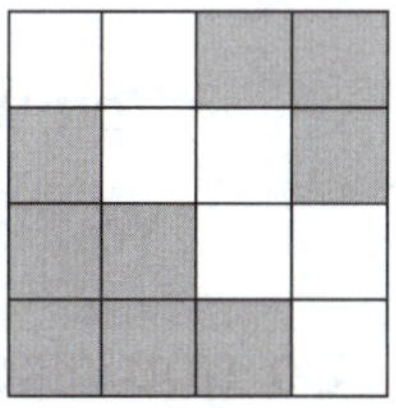

a) Which two shapes have the same fraction shaded?

b) What fraction do these two shapes have shaded?

9 For every 3 hours Petra spends practising her banjo she is allowed to spend 1 hour watching TV.

This week Petra has practised her banjo for 6 hours.
How long is she allowed to watch TV for?

10 1 in every 6 of Max's apples is red. He has 12 apples altogether.

How many red apples does Max have?

11 Bob wants to **estimate** the **sum** and **difference** of 17 and 89.
Write down the calculation he could do in each case.

a) The sum of 17 and 89.

b) The difference between 17 and 89.

Adding and Subtracting

Adding Multiples of 10, 100 and 1000

Multiples of 10, 100 and 1000 all have zeros at the end.

To add them, use number facts you already know.

For example, you know sums like this. → 7 + 2 = 9

So you also know all these sums. →

70 + 20 = 90

700 + 200 = 900

7000 + 2000 = 9000

The same number of zeros have been added to each number.

EXAMPLE: Find the missing number: "9000 is one thousand less than ☐."

You want to find: 9000 + 1000 = ?

You know that: → 9 + 1 = 10

So you also know that: 9 thousand + 1 thousand = 10 thousand

So 9000 is one thousand less than 10 000.

Subtracting Multiples of 10, 100 and 1000

You can do the same thing with subtractions.

EXAMPLE: 3000 – 700 – 600 = ?

Make an easier calculation. Here all the numbers are 100 times smaller. (Two zeros have been taken off each number.)

30 – 7 – 6 = 17

Now make the numbers 100 times bigger again.

3000 – 700 – 600 = 1700

EXAMPLE: Subtract one hundred and eighty from one thousand.

Write out the problem in numbers. → 1000 – 180 = ?

Make an easier calculation. The numbers are ten times smaller.

100 – 18 = 82

Make the numbers 10 times bigger again.

1000 – 180 = 820

Learning Objective:

"I can work out sums and differences of multiples of 10, 100 or 1000."

Adding and Subtracting

Question 1

Fiona collects stamps. She has **30** already. On her birthday, Fiona receives **80** stamps from her sister and **140** stamps from her aunt. How many stamps does Fiona have altogether?

1. You need to add up the numbers of stamps.
2. The numbers are all multiples of ten. You can make an easier calculation using number facts you know by making the numbers 10 times smaller.
3. Make the numbers 10 times bigger again.
4. Make sure you answer the question.

30 + 80 + 140

3 + 8 + 14
= 11 + 14
= 25

So 30 + 80 + 140 = 250

So Fiona has 250 stamps altogether.

Question 2

Lucy has 2000 stickers. She uses 600 of them. How many stickers does she have left?

1. You need to subtract 600 stickers from 2000 stickers.
2. 2000 and 600 are both multiples of 100 so make them both 100 times smaller. Write the subtraction out showing this. (You can't do 2 thousands – 6 hundreds. The multiples have to match.)
3. Now work out the easy calculation. Then make the numbers 100 times bigger again.

2000 – 600 = ?

20 hundreds – 6 hundreds = ?
20 – 6 = ?

20 – 6 = 14
So 2000 – 600 = 1400

Lucy has 1400 stickers left.

Use number facts to make easier calculations...

If you need to add multiples of 10, 100 or 1000, e.g. 400 + 600, don't panic. Think of easy number pairs that you know. You know that 4 + 6 = 10, so 400 + 600 = 1000.

Checking Calculations

Do the Inverse to Check Your Answers

You can check a calculation by doing the opposite calculation — this is called the inverse calculation.

EXAMPLE: 100 – 32 = 68. Write down the addition you would do to check this answer is right.

ANSWER: 68 + 32 = 100

Addition is the inverse of subtraction.

EXAMPLE: 21 ÷ 3 = 7. Write down a calculation you could do to check this answer is right.

ANSWER: 3 × 7 = 21

The inverse of division is multiplication.

You can also Estimate to Check Your Answers

You can also check a calculation by estimating the answer. If your estimate is very different from your 'proper' answer then your proper answer is probably wrong.

EXAMPLE: Find 92 – 13.

Do it: 92 – 13 = 79

Check it: 92 – 13 is almost the same as 90 – 10.

90 – 10 = 80.

80 is very close to 79. So your answer is probably right.

90 – 10 is easy to do. You can quickly check your answer is about right.

EXAMPLE: Tom says "11 times 3 is 29". Is he right?

You know 10 × 3 = 30 from the 3 times table.

11 is bigger than 10.

So 11 × 3 should be bigger than 30.

So Tom is wrong.

Learning Objective:

"I can estimate and check my calculations."

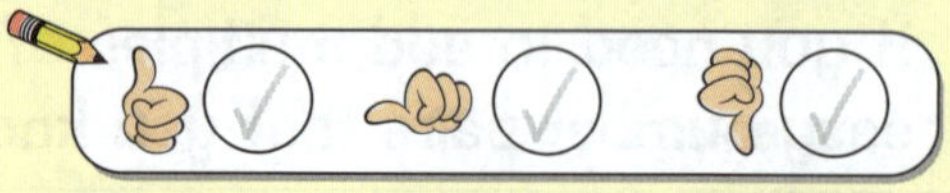

Checking Calculations

Question 1

Alice works out that 67 + 26 = 83.
Check her answer by doing an inverse calculation.
Show your **working** and say whether Alice's answer is **right** or **wrong**.

1. Write down the inverse calculation. The inverse of "add 26" is "subtract 26".
2. Solve the inverse calculation.
3. Compare your answer to the other number in Alice's calculation.

Alice: 67 + 26 = 83
Inverse calculation: 83 – 26 = ?

83 – 26 = 83 – 20 – 6
= 63 – 6
= 57

67 + 26 = 83.
83 – 26 = 57, not 67.
Alice's answer is wrong.

Question 2

Toby says, "13 lots of 4 apples is 38 apples." Is he correct?
Use estimation to work out your answer.

1. Write down what calculation the question is asking you about.
2. Think of an easier calculation that is close to Toby's calculation. You know 10 × 4 from your 4 times table, so solve that.
3. Compare your estimate to Toby's answer. 13 is greater than 10, so Toby's answer should be greater than 40.
4. Answer the question.

13 lots of 4 apples is 38 apples
13 × 4 = 38

10 × 4 = 40

Toby's answer = 38 apples
Estimate = 40 apples
Toby's answer is less than the estimate.

Toby's answer is too small, so he is wrong.

An inverse calculation is the opposite calculation...

You can do an estimate to check your answer. But make sure you use an easy calculation that's quick to do. Then if the 'proper' answer is close to your estimate, it's probably right.

Multiplication and Division

You Need to Know Your Times Tables

You can work out your times tables on number lines.

Here's the 2 times table.
The numbers go up in steps of two.

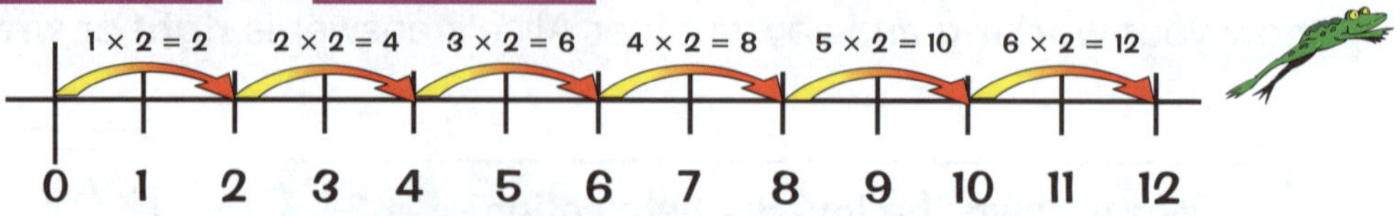

You need to learn your 3, 4, 5, 6 and 10 times tables as well.

Multiplication is the Same as "Times"

3 lots of 7 or 3 groups of 7 is the same as "3 times 7" or "3 × 7".
The maths word for this is multiplication.

EXAMPLE: Betty has 2 groups of 4 cats.

This is the same as 2 × 4.
From the 2 times table you know that 2 × 4 = 8. So Betty has 8 cats.

Division is the opposite of multiplication.

EXAMPLE: Divide 6 bananas between 3 monkeys.

Split the bananas into 3 groups. Each monkey gets 2 bananas.

This is the same as 6 ÷ 3 = 2.

Multiples are Just Like Times Tables

Multiples of 2 are just the numbers in the 2 times table:

2 4 6 8 10 12 14 16 ...

Multiples of 2 are even numbers. They end in 0, 2, 4, 6 or 8.

It's easy to remember: multiples are just multiplication tables.

The multiples of 5 are 5 10 15 20 25 30 ...

Multiples of 5 all end in zero or 5.

The multiples of 10 are 10 20 30 40 50 60 ...

Multiples of 10 all end in zero.

Learning Objective:

"I know my tables for 2, 3, 4, 5, 6 and 10 and their division facts. I can recognise multiples of 2, 5 and 10."

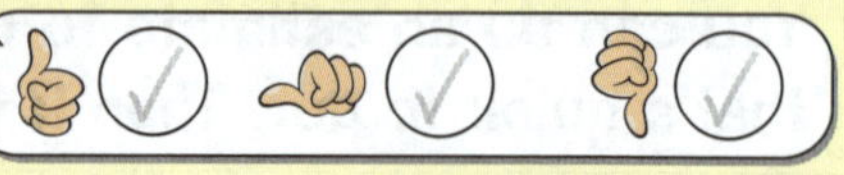

Multiplication and Division

Question 1

a) **Seven** children eat **five** fairy cakes each. How many cakes do they eat altogether?
b) **£54** is shared between **six** friends. How much money does each person get?

a You need to work out 7 × 5. This is the same as 5 × 7. So you can use the 5 times table or the 7 times table.

b) **1** You have to divide 54 by 6. Multiplication is the opposite of division, so think of your 6 times table. You need to find ? × 6 = 54.

2 You know that 9 × 6 = 54, so 54 ÷ 6 must be 9. Answer the question in pounds.

a) 5 × 7 = 7 × 5 = 35 cakes

b) 7 × 6 = 42
8 × 6 = 48
9 × 6 = 54

54 ÷ 6 = 9
So each person gets £9.

Question 2

Which **three** of these numbers add to make a multiple of 5? 2 4 7 9

1 You're trying to make a multiple of 5 — a number that ends in 0 or 5. So try adding any three of the numbers first, e.g. 2 + 4 + 7. The answer to this is 13. It's not a multiple of 5 because it doesn't end in 0 or 5.

2 Next, try adding a different three numbers together e.g. 2 + 4 + 9. The answer to this is 15 — it ends in 5 so it is a multiple of 5.

3 Write down the answer to the question.

2 + 4 + 7
= 6 + 7
= 13 — no good

2 + 4 + 9
= 6 + 9
= 15 — good

The 3 numbers are 2, 4 and 9. (4, 7 and 9 would also be correct.)

Multiples of 5 are numbers in the 5 times table...

Make sure you know how to spot multiples of 2 (they are even), multiples of 5 (they end in 0 or 5) and multiples of 10 (they end in 0). And remember to learn your times tables.

Practice Questions

1 Joe writes down the results of an onion throwing contest:

200 m 600 m 20 m 300 m 900 m 130 m 400 m 50 m

Which three scores add up to 1100 m?

2 Copy this diagram.
Draw lines to join all the pairs of number cards that have a difference of 40.

One has been done for you.

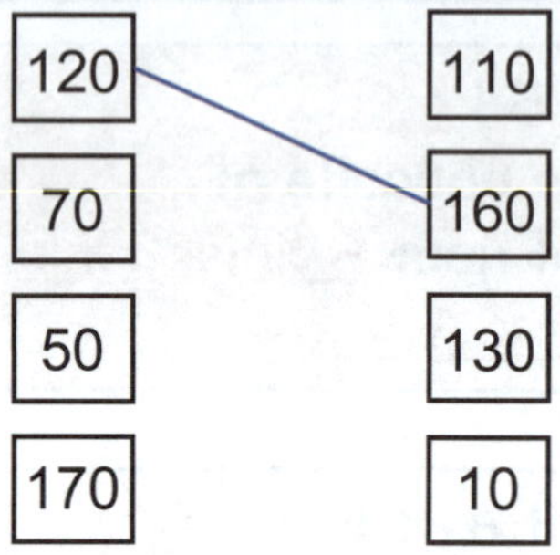

3 What is 150 – 60 – 30?

4 Jenny is playing a computer game. She gains 50 points on Level 1 and 80 points on Level 2. But on Level 3 she loses 70 points.

How many points does Jenny have altogether?

5 Ellen works out that 21 + 79 is 100.
Her teacher says, 'Do an inverse calculation to check your answer.'

Write down the calculation Ellen should do.

6 Check Tasha's answers using inverse calculations.
Show your **working** and say whether she is **right** or **wrong** in each case.

a) 35 + 42 = 77 b) 36 ÷ 4 = 8 c) 81 – 36 = 45

7 What are the missing numbers in these calculations?

a) 35 + □ = 100 b) 8 × □ = 48 c) □ ÷ 4 = 9

8 Copy this number sentence. Write numbers in the boxes to make it correct.

58 + □ – □ = 58

Practice Questions

9 Anna works out that 122 – 43 is 65.

Use estimation to check her answer. Is Anna's answer likely to be right or wrong?

10 Phil the postman has 23 sacks of parcels. Each sack contains 5 parcels.

Estimate how many parcels Phil has altogether.

11 What is six multiplied by nine?

12 Sarah has 4 female dogs. Each dog has 6 puppies.

How many dogs does Sarah now have altogether?

13 Dave has 42 chocolates.
He shares the chocolates out equally between himself and 5 friends.

How many chocolates does each person get?

14 John has eight 5-pence pieces.

a) How much money does John have altogether?

b) Is the answer a multiple of 10? Explain your answer.

15 Write down the numbers from this grid that are multiples of 2.

27	32	31	38	45
25	44	42	30	23
33	34	36	43	28

16 Write down **three** of these numbers that add to make a multiple of 5.

6 7 8 9 10 11

Mental Maths

Add or Subtract by Partitioning...

Adding or subtracting two-digit numbers in your head can be hard.
You can partition one number into its tens and units to make it easier.

46 + 57 = ?

This looks tricky. So try partitioning the 57.

46 + 57 is the same as 46 + 50 + 7."

Boris the whizz-pig

46 + 50 = 96

96 + 7 = 103

So 46 + 57 = 103

You can also subtract two-digit numbers this way.

94 – 36 = ?

94 – 30 = 64...

... 64 – 6 = 58

...Or Make an Easier Calculation First

Another way is to use a near, easy number and then adjust your answer.

EXAMPLE: What is 73 – 37?

37 is close to 40, so subtract 40 instead of 37 — then add 3 back on because you took away 3 too many.

You can add numbers this way too.

73 – 40 = 33....

... 33 + 3 = 36...

... So 73 – 37 = 36.

Learning Objective:

"I can add or subtract two-digit whole numbers in my head."

Mental Maths

Question 1

In a field there are **33** white sheep and **48** black sheep.

a) How many sheep are there altogether?

b) **16** white sheep escape from the field. How many white sheep are there now?

a)

1. You need to add the numbers of white sheep and black sheep together.
2. Partition the 48 into 4 tens and 8 units.
3. Add 4 tens to 33. Then add 8 units to this answer. Write out the final answer clearly.

a) 33 + 48

33 + 40 + 8

33 + 40 = 73

73 + 8 = 81

So there are 81 sheep.

b)

1. You need to subtract 16 from 33.
2. Partition the 16 into 1 ten and 6 units.
3. Subtract the ten from 33, then subtract the units. Write out the answer clearly.

b) 33 – 16

33 – 10 – 6

33 – 10 = 23

23 – 6 = 17

There are 17 white sheep now.

Question 2

Jeremy wants to buy some stickers for 54p and a chocolate bar for 38p.
How much will these cost altogether?

1. You need to work out 54p + 38p. You can make this easier by adding 40 to 54, then subtracting 2, because you added 2 too many.
2. Solve the calculation and answer the question clearly. Make sure you write your answer in pence.

54 + 38

= 54 + 40 – 2

54 + 40 = 94

94 – 2 = 92

So they will cost 92p in total.

Partitioning makes calculations easier...

If you need to add or subtract two-digit numbers in your head, don't panic. You can use partitioning. Or you can make an easier sum first, solve that and then adjust your answer.

Written Adding and Subtracting

You Can Add in Columns...

This is a good way to add big numbers.
You can use it to add up the units, tens and hundreds separately.

EXAMPLE: What is 384 + 165?

ANSWER:

```
  H T U
  3 8 4
+ 1 6 5
-------
      9
+   140
+   400
-------
    549
```

Write one number on top of the other, lining up the units.

1) First, add the units. 4 + 5 = 9

2) Then add the tens. 80 + 60 = 140

3) Then add the hundreds. 300 + 100 = 400

4) Finally, add up the columns.

So 384 + 165 = 549

...and You Can Subtract in Columns

It's easier to subtract the units, tens and hundreds of a number separately.

EXAMPLE: Clarice has £8.04 but she spends £4.51 on earrings.
How much money does she have left?

Remember, £1 = 100p.

You can change the amounts into pence first, to make whole numbers.
The calculation you have to do is 804p – 451p.

Partition 451 into hundreds, tens and units. → 451 = 400 + 50 + 1

"804 – 400 – 50 – 1" → Start with 804.

Subtract 1

...then 50

...then 400

```
  804
−   1
-----
  803
−  50
-----
  753
− 400
-----
  353
```

Remember to change the answer back into pounds and pence.

So Clarice has £3.53 left.

Learning Objective:

"I can add or subtract two-digit and three-digit whole numbers using efficient written methods."

Written Adding and Subtracting

Question 1

Phil buys a magazine for **£2.85** and a drink for **76p**. How much does he pay altogether?

1. Change £2.85 into pence (so that both amounts are in pence).
2. Then write the calculation in columns with the units lined up.
3. Now add the numbers. Add the units first, then the tens, then the hundreds.
4. Then add the three totals — 11 + 150 + 200.
5. Finally, answer the question in pounds and pence.

£2.85 = 285p

```
  285
+  76
-----
```

```
  285
+  76
-----
   11  <—— 5 + 6
+ 150  <—— 80 + 70
+ 200  <—— 200 + 0
-----
  361
```

Phil pays £3.61 altogether.

Question 2

Amy has **683** honey bees. She gives **457** of these bees to a friend.
How many bees does she have left?

1. You need to work out 683 – 457.
   Partition 457 into hundreds, tens and units.
2. Now subtract the numbers in three steps:
   1) Subtract the units from 683.
      683 – 7 = 676
   2) Subtract the tens from that answer.
      676 – 50 = 626
   3) Subtract the hundreds. 626 – 400 = 226
3. Now answer the question.

683 – 457
457 = 400 + 50 + 7

```
  683
–   7
-----
  676
–  50
-----
  626
– 400
-----
  226
-----
```

Amy has 226 bees left.

Add or subtract the units first...

If a question is in '£' and 'p' you can change everything into pence first. Then you do the calculation in pence. Then just change the answer back to pounds and pence at the end.

Written Multiplying and Dividing

You Can Multiply Using a Grid

In this method, you multiply in easy steps.

EXAMPLE: Work out 26 × 5.

1) Draw a grid like this.

2) Put the number you're multiplying by at the top.

3) Partition the other number into tens and units.
26 = 20 + 6
Put the 20 and the 6 on the left.

×	5
20	100
6	30
	130

4) Now fill in the grid. Multiply the number at the top by each number on the left.

20 × 5 = 100
(You know that 2 × 5 = 10. So you know that 20 × 5 = 100.)

6 × 5 = 30

5) Add your answers together.

100 + 30 = 130

So, 26 × 5 = 130

Divide by Splitting Big Numbers into Parts

If big numbers aren't in times tables you know, then split them up.

EXAMPLE: Work out 54 ÷ 3.

Because you're dividing by 3.

1) Partition 54 into multiples of 3. For example, 54 = 30 + 24.

2) Now divide 30 and 24 by 3.

You can work these out from your times tables.
3 × 10 = 30 and 3 × 8 = 24

54 ÷ 3 = 30 ÷ 3 + 24 ÷ 3
= 10 + 8 = 18

Sometimes You get a Remainder

Some numbers don't divide exactly. You get some left over. This is a remainder.

EXAMPLE: Work out 87 ÷ 5.

87 ÷ 5 = 50 ÷ 5 + 37 ÷ 5
= 10 + 7 r2 = 17 r2

5 doesn't go into 37 exactly, but you know that 7 × 5 = 35. So 5 goes into 37 7 times with 2 left over (remainder of 2).

Add 7 r2 to 10 to find the answer.
87 ÷ 5 = 10 + 7 r2 = 17 r2.

Learning Objective:

"I can multiply and divide a two-digit number by a one-digit number. I can find the remainder."

Written Multiplying and Dividing

Question 1

Tom has **7** bags of toffees. There are **48** toffees in each bag.
How many toffees does he have altogether?

1. Draw a grid. Put 7 at the top. Partition 48 into 40 + 8 then put these down the left hand side.

×	7
40	
8	

2. Fill in the grid in three steps:
   1) Multiply 7 by 40. You know that 7 × 4 = 28, so 7 × 40 = 280.
   2) Multiply 7 by 8. 7 × 8 = 56
   3) Add the answers. 280 + 56 = 336

×	7
40	280
8	56
	336

3. Write out the answer clearly.

Tom has 336 toffees altogether.

Question 2

Work out **79 ÷ 6**.

1. Partition 79 into multiples of 6. You know that 6 × 10 = 60. This leaves 19. 19 isn't a multiple of 6, so this division will have a remainder.

79 = 60 + 19

You can estimate the answer first. 79 is between 60 and 120 so the answer must be between 60 ÷ 6 (= 10) and 120 ÷ 6 (= 20).

2. Divide 60 and 19 by 6. 19 doesn't divide exactly by 6, but you know that 3 × 6 = 18. So 6 goes into 19 3 times with a remainder of 1.

60 ÷ 6 = 10

19 ÷ 6 = 3 r1

3. Add your answers together to get the final answer.

10 + 3 r1 = 13 r1

So 79 ÷ 6 = 13 r1.

Your times tables help you with dividing too...

Remember, when you're multiplying you partition the 'big number' into tens and units. But when you're dividing, you partition the 'big number' into multiples of the small number.

Calculators

How to Use a Calculator

1) Make sure it says '0' before you start.
2) Press the buttons carefully.
3) Always check the display to make sure you've pressed the right button.
4) Press the [=] button at the end of every calculation.

Learn Where the Cancel Button Is

Find out which button cancels the last number you typed in.

It's usually [CE] or [C] (or [DEL] on some calculators).

Ask your teacher if you're not sure.

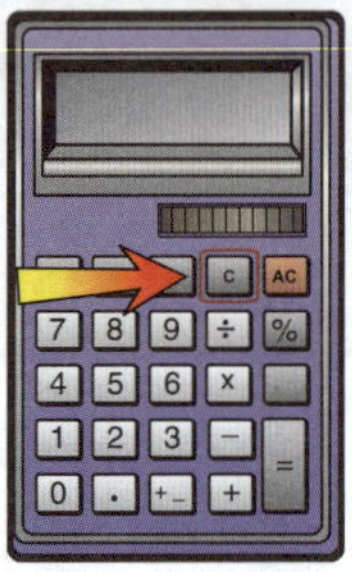

Don't Just Copy the Display

Make sure you know what the answer on your calculator means.

EXAMPLE: James has £2.27. He spends 97p. How much does he have left?

Change the 97p into pounds, so that both amounts are in the same units.

So type in: [2] [.] [2] [7] [−] [0] [.] [9] [7] [=] → display: 1.3

But you wouldn't ever write £1.3 — you always use 2 decimal places for pence. So you need to put a zero on the end... £1.30

You'd get the same answer if you changed £2.27 into pence.

Recognising Negative Numbers...

EXAMPLE: The temperature of some slime is 21.4 °C. Dr Chillwell heats the slime up by 65.9 °C. Then she cools it by 237.19 °C. What is the temperature of the slime now?

Do this calculation using your calculator: 21.4 + 65.9 − 237.19

The display will read: -149.89

Don't forget the negative sign.

The temperature of the slime is −149.89 °C.

Learning Objective:

"I can use a calculator to help me solve problems."

Calculators

Question 1

Ellie and her **three brothers** have **£15** to **share** equally between them.
Ellie buys a book for **£2.79**. How much money does Ellie have left, in pence?

1. You need to divide £15 by 4 (Ellie and her 3 brothers), using your calculator.

2. You now know that Ellie gets **£3.75**. She spends **£2.79**. So now subtract **£2.79** from **£3.75**.

3. Convert **£0.96** into pence (the question says to give the answer in pence).

15 ÷ 4 = 3.75 = £3.75

3.75 – 2.79 = 0.96
That's £0.96.

£0.96 = 96p
Ellie has 96p left.

Question 2

James has a cup of milk. The temperature of the milk is 5.6 °C. James heats the milk up by 78 °C. Then he puts it in the snow outside. The milk cools down by 101.8 °C.
What is the temperature of the milk now?

1. The milk starts off at 5.6 °C. Then the temperature goes up by 78 °C. So you need to add 78 to 5.6

2. Now the temperature goes down by 101.8 °C. You need to subtract.

3. Remember to give the correct unit in your answer.

5.6 + 78 = 83.6

83.6 – 101.8 = –18.2

The temperature of the milk is now –18.2 °C

Make sure you know what buttons to press...

Calculators can be a big help, but you still have to decide what calculations to do. Then you have to work out what the answer on the display means, and write it down properly.

Practice Questions

1 How much less is thirty-five than eighty-two? Work it out in your head.

2 Sam has 32 sweets. He eats 15 of them.

How many does he have left? Work it out in your head.

3 Kelly is 37 years younger than her mum. Kelly is 12 years old.

How old is Kelly's mum? Work it out in your head.

4 Phil buys a hat for £3.25 and a pair of gloves for £1.44

How much does he spend altogether?

5 Darren buys an armchair for £145 and a sofa for £289.

How much does he spend altogether?

6 Calculate 224 – 187.

7 Here is a chip shop's price list.

a) Adil buys some chips and a cup of tea.
How much does he pay?

b) Pete buys fish and chips and a can of cola.
How much does he pay?

Food		Drinks	
Chips	£1.05	Tea	65p
Fish and Chips	£3.20	Coffee	75p
Pie and Chips	£2.69	Can of cola	54p
Sausage	98p	Orange Juice	78p

8 Divide eighty by five.

9 Jill makes 46 iced buns. She shares them equally between six friends but there are some buns left over.

How many iced buns are left over?

Practice Questions

10 Dean spends 55p on bus fares every day for four days.

How much does he spend altogether?

11 Find the missing numbers to make these calculations correct.

a) $4 \times 60 = \square$ b) $45 \div 3 = \square$

12 Ruby wants to buy a sandwich for £3.75

She has £1.34
How much more money does she need?

13 A family of two adults and one child go to the zoo.

How much do they pay altogether?

Zoo Entry Prices	
Adults	£17.50
Children	£10.00

14 Complete this two digit number so it is a multiple of 3.

	1

15 Muffins are sold in packs of 6.

Lara wants 192 muffins. How many packs must she buy?

16 Chocolate bars cost 46p each. Ada buys 3 chocolate bars.

Ada pays with a £2 coin.
How much change does she get?

17 A scientist measures the temperature of some water. It is 34.7 °C.

He heats the water by 62.7 °C. He then puts it in a freezer and it cools down by 106.8 °C.
What is the temperature of the water now?

2D Shapes

"2D" means 2 dimensional. A 2D shape is flat — it has length and width but no thickness.

A Polygon is a 2D Shape with Straight Sides

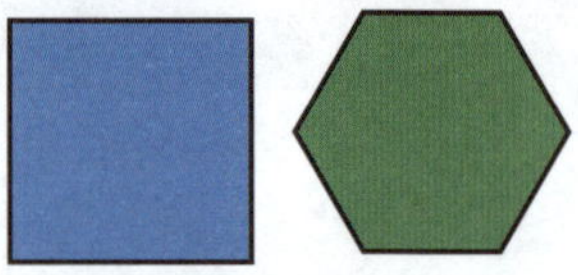

Be careful when you draw polygons. Make sure all the lines meet up.

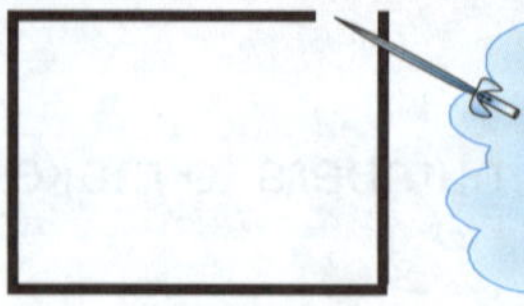

This isn't a polygon. The lines don't meet at the top corner.

Regular Polygons Have Sides of Equal Length

The name of a polygon tells you how many sides and angles it has.

Regular pentagon
5 equal sides.
5 equal angles.

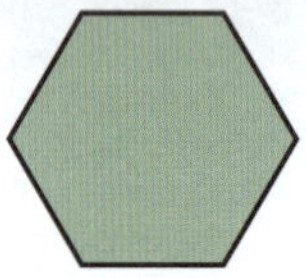

Regular hexagon
6 equal sides.
6 equal angles.

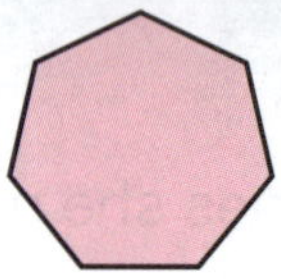

Regular heptagon
7 equal sides.
7 equal angles.

Regular octagon
8 equal sides.
8 equal angles.

These polygons are irregular. Their sides are not all the same length.

These are irregular hexagons. They each have 6 sides.

Quadrilaterals are Polygons with Four Sides

Squares and oblongs are both types of rectangle.

4 equal sides.
4 right angles.

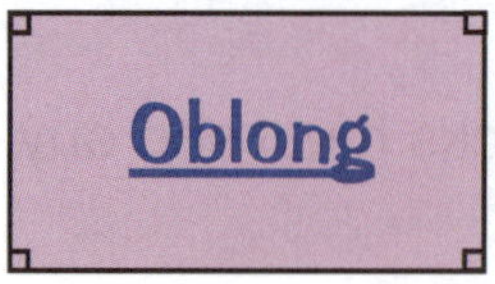

2 pairs of equal sides.
4 right angles.

A right angle is just a quarter turn.

There are Different Types of Triangle

Equilateral triangle
3 sides of equal length.
3 equal angles.

Isosceles triangle
2 sides of equal length.
2 equal angles.

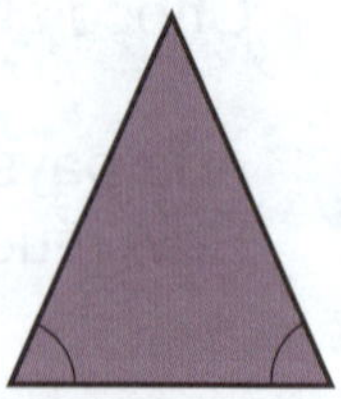

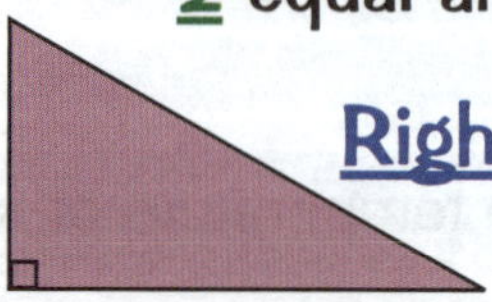

Right-angled triangle
1 angle is a right angle.

Learning Objective:

"I know facts about regular polygons such as the number of sides and number of angles."

2D Shapes

Question 1

Dave has made a table about the properties of shapes.
Fill in the gaps to complete his table.

	Number of sides	Number of right angles
Equilateral triangle		
Regular octagon		
Oblong		
Regular hexagon		

1. Imagine each shape and count the number of sides. Write the answers in the correct boxes of the table.

2. Then, work out if there are any right angles in each shape. Fill in the numbers in the table.

	Number of sides	Number of right angles
Equilateral triangle	3	0
Regular octagon	8	0
Oblong	4	4
Regular hexagon	6	0

Question 2

On the grid, draw two more lines to complete the square.

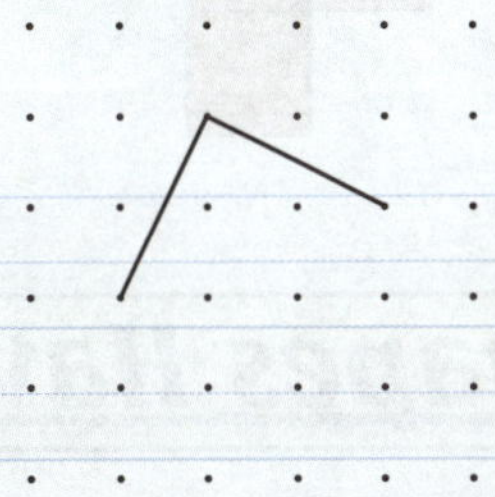

1. Think about what you know about squares.

2. Use what you know to draw in the final two sides of the square.

3. It's a good idea to use a set-square to check that all the angles are 90°.

Squares have 4 sides of equal length.
They also have 4 right angles.

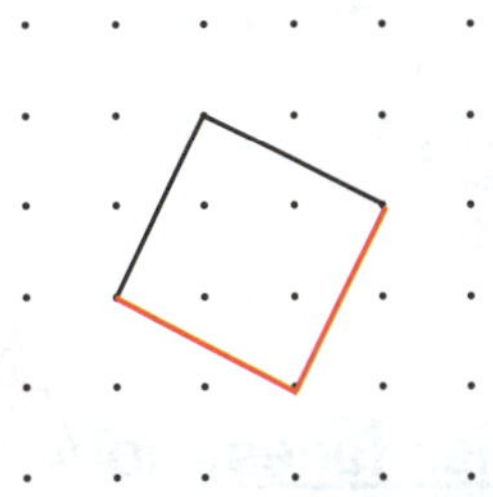

You can group polygons based on their properties...

Don't get regular and irregular polygons mixed up. All the sides of a regular polygon are the same length and all its angles are the same. For example, a square is a regular quadrilateral.

3D Shapes

A Shape Net Folds Up to Make a 3D Shape

If you take a cardboard box apart you're left with the net.

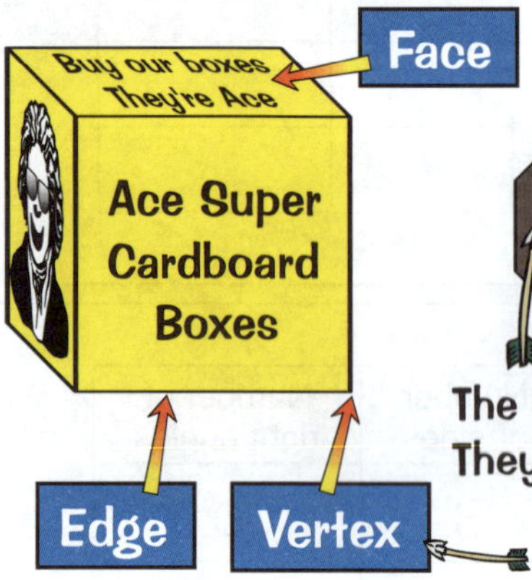

The flaps are used for gluing the box together.
They're not part of the net.

Vertices means corners.
You say it "verti-sees".

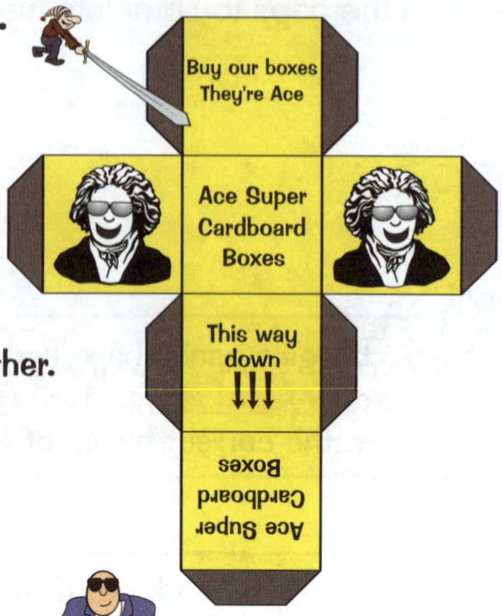

There's more than one net for a cube.
Here are some examples:

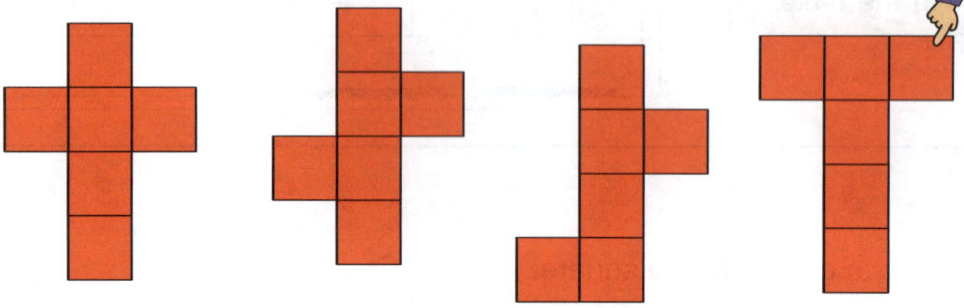

You just fold along the lines to make the cube.

All 3D Shapes Have Nets

All 3D shapes have nets.

Each face of the 3D shape has to match up with one part of the net.

Triangular Prism

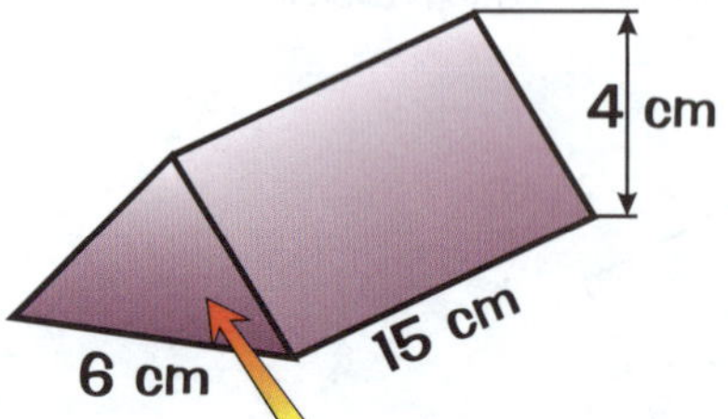

There are 2 triangular faces, so 2 parts of the net must be triangles.

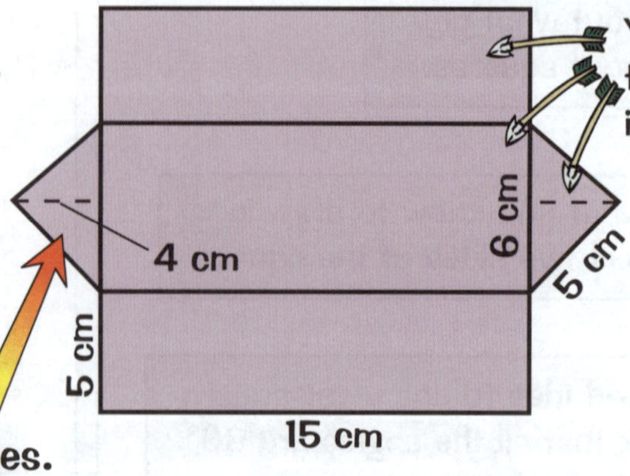

You can't see these three faces in the 3D picture.

Learning Objective:

"When I look at a drawing of a 3D shape I can work out what shapes I need to make its net."

3D Shapes

Question 1

Anne is making the net of a triangular prism. Complete it by drawing in the lines that she must fold along.

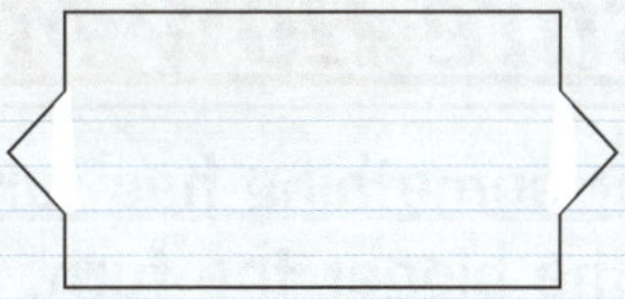

1. Work out what shaped faces a triangular prism has.

2. Draw lines to split the net up into these shapes.

A triangular prism has 3 rectangular faces and 2 triangular faces.

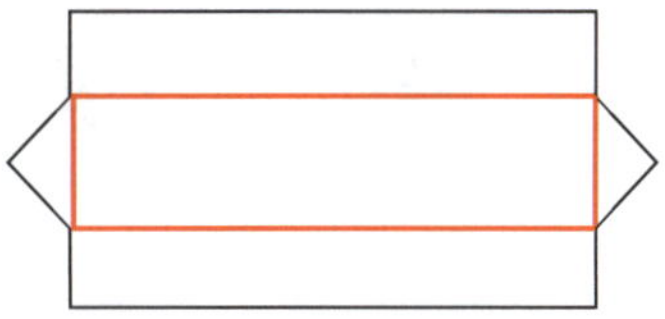

Question 2

Ahmed draws a table to show the properties of some 3D shapes. Complete his table.

	number of edges	number of vertices
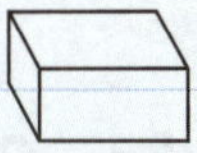 cuboid		
 square-based pyramid		

1. Count the number of edges. You can't see both sides of the shapes, so imagine the edges you can't see. If you find it easier, you could draw in the hidden sides.

2. Then count the vertices on each shape. These are just the corners. Don't forget about the ones that you can't see in the diagrams.

	number of edges	number of vertices
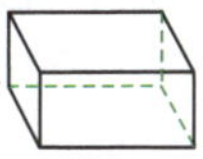 cuboid	12	8
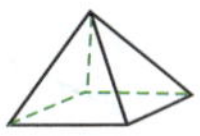 square-based pyramid	8	5

All 3D shapes have nets...

If you're struggling to work out a net, try drawing it on paper and then folding it up. If it makes a solid shape with no faces missing, then you've probably got it right.

Angles

Angles Measure How Much Something Turns

Angles tell you how far something has turned.
The bigger the angle, the bigger the turn.
Turns are measured in degrees (°).

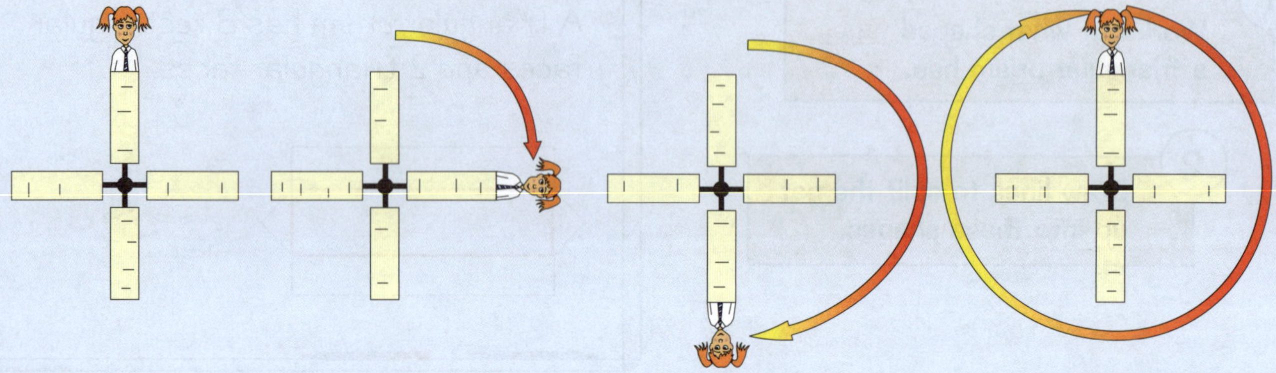

A quarter turn is 90 degrees. You can also call them right angles.

A half turn is 180 degrees. It's the same as 2 right angles.

A full turn is 360 degrees. It's the same as 4 right angles.

EXAMPLE: Give an angle that is smaller than 2 right angles but bigger than one right angle.

One right angle is 90°. Two right angles are 180°.
So you could give any angle over 90° but less than 180°, for example, 102°.

EXAMPLE: Look at the angles below. Circle the smallest angle. One of the angles is bigger than a right angle. Put a tick next to it.

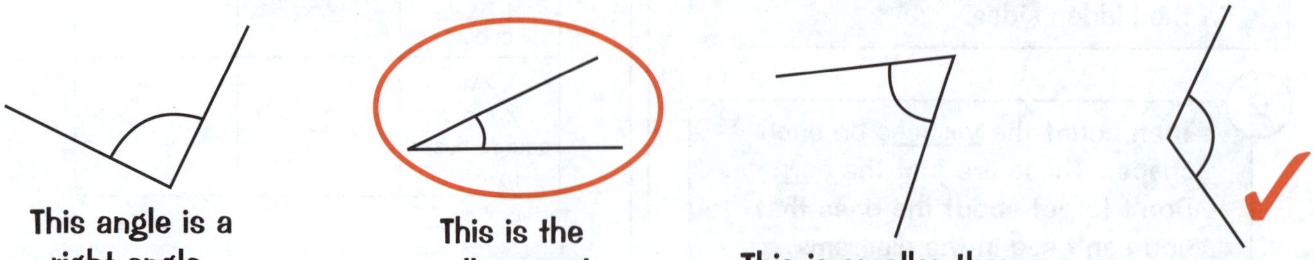

This angle is a right angle.

This is the smallest angle.

This is smaller than a right angle but it's not the smallest.

This is bigger than a right angle.

Learning Objective:

"I can compare and order angles."

Angles

Question 1

Harry draws some angles.

a) How many of the angles are smaller than a right angle?

b) Put a tick next to any right angles.

a) 1. Right angles are quarter turns. They measure 90°.

2. Circle the angles that are smaller than this and then count them up.

b) 1. Look for any angles that are exactly a quarter turn.

2. You can double check your answer using a protractor (angle measurer) if you're not sure.

a)

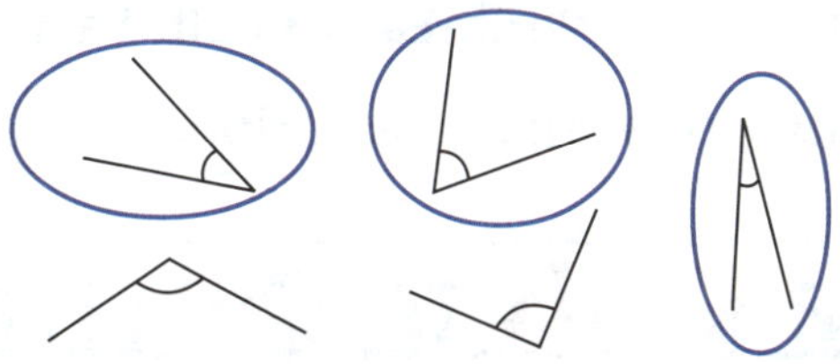

So there are 3 angles that are smaller than a right angle.

b)

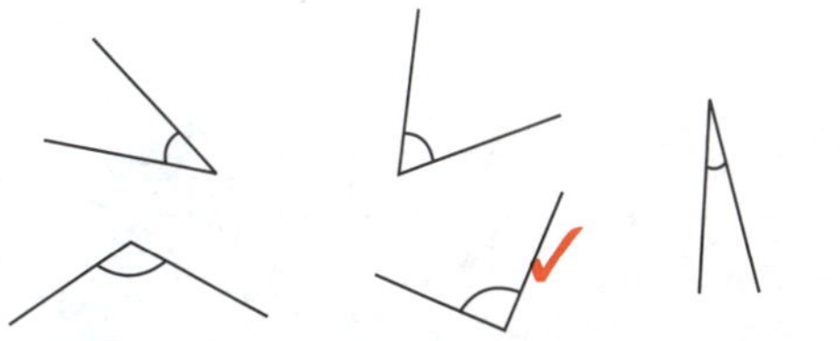

Question 2

Alfred's game comes with the spinner on the right. Which direction will the arrow be pointing in if it turns through 180°? Circle the correct letter.

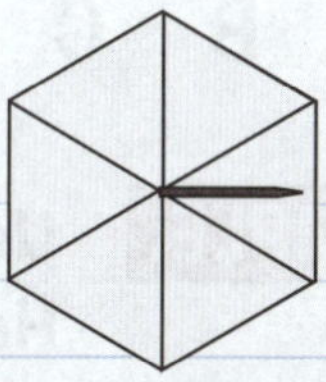

A 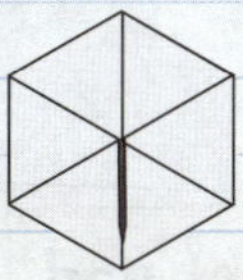 B 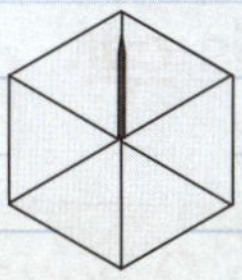 C 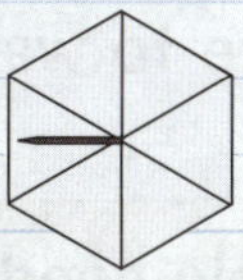

1. 180° is a half turn or two right angles.

2. Look at each spinner to see which arrow has turned by 180°.

A has only made a quarter turn (90°).

B has made a quarter turn in the other direction.

This leaves spinner C —
C has made a half turn.

There are 4 right angles in a full turn...

Make sure you can remember what quarter turns (90°) and half turns (180°) look like. If you have to estimate the size of an angle, it helps to compare it with these angles.

Coordinates

North, South, East and West

The four main compass directions are North, South, East and West.

There are also the halfway directions:
North-East, South-East, South-West and North-West.

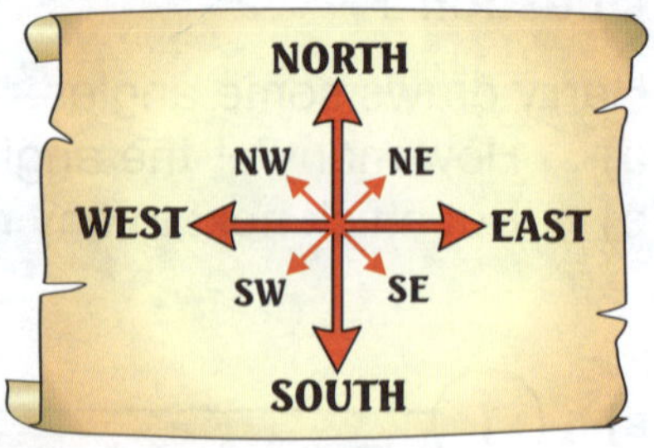

You can use these directions to say which way you're facing.

Use Grids to Describe Where Things Are

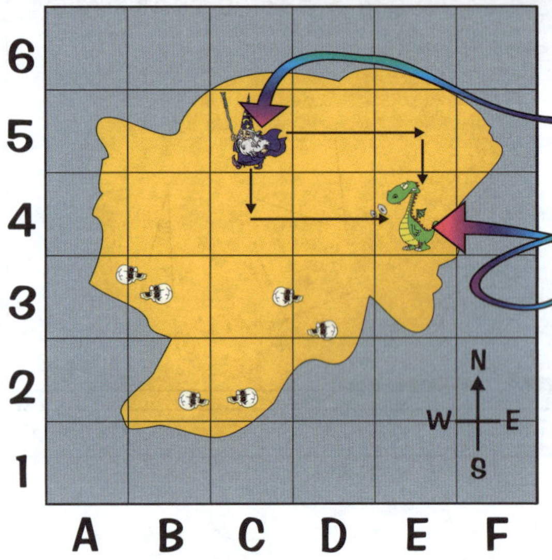

Read down from the object to the letter.
Then read across to the number.
The wizard is in square C5. Easy.

The dragon is in square E4.
To reach the dragon, the wizard has to go 1 square down (south) and 2 squares to the right (east).

Or, he can go 2 squares to the right (east) and then 1 square down (south).

EXAMPLE: Use compass directions to describe the route Herman Hamster should take to walk to his car.

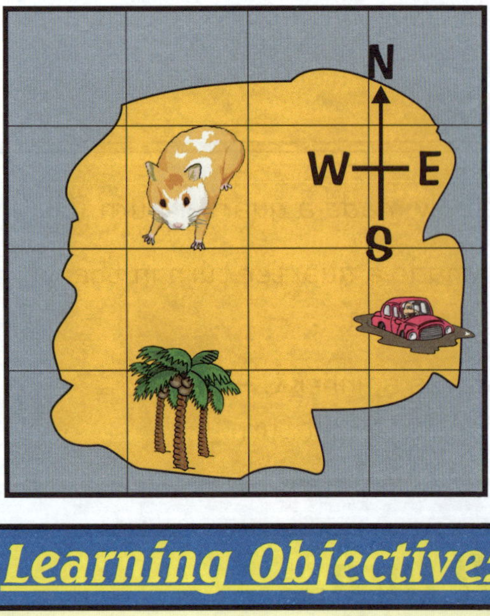

He needs to go 2 squares east and 1 square south to reach his car.

Once he has got to his car, how can he get to the trees?

He needs to go 2 squares west and 1 square south to get to the trees.

Learning Objective:

"I can describe compass directions and the position of a square on a grid."

Coordinates

Question 1

Luke moves his counter 3 squares right and 4 squares up.
What are the coordinates of its new position?

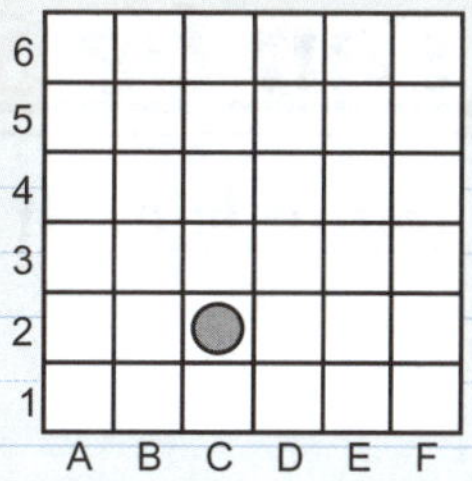

1. Draw the path that the counter takes.
It moves 3 squares right
then 4 squares up.

2. Work out the coordinates.
Read down to the letter at the bottom and the number on the left.

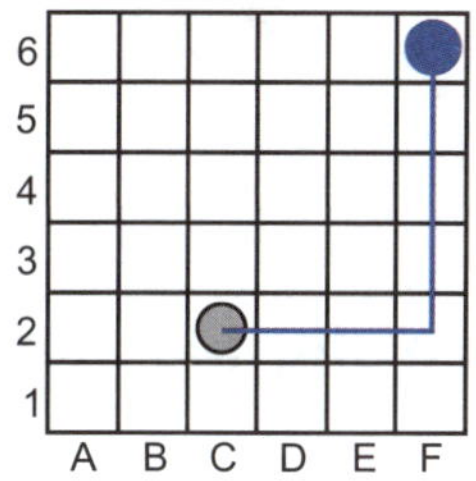

The counter is now in square F6.

Question 2

Sasha is at square B3 on the map.

a) She is facing **north-west**. She turns through **90° clockwise**.
What direction is she facing now?

b) Sasha wants to move from square B3 to square E5.
Use **compass directions** to describe how she could do this.

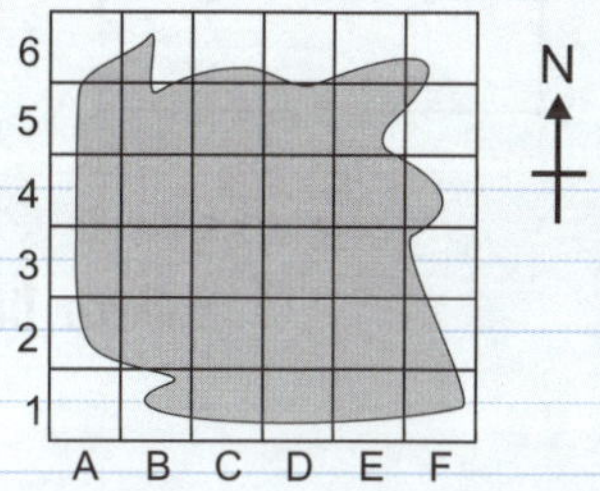

a) Draw out the 8 compass directions.
Put an arrow showing north-west.
Then turn the arrow through a quarter turn clockwise.

b)

1. Mark the two squares on the grid.

2. Work out a way of getting from B3 to E5. Count how many squares east/west then how many north/south.

a)

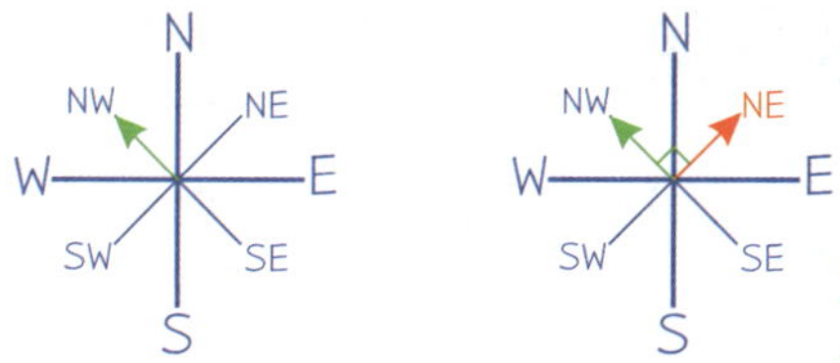

She is facing north-east.

b)

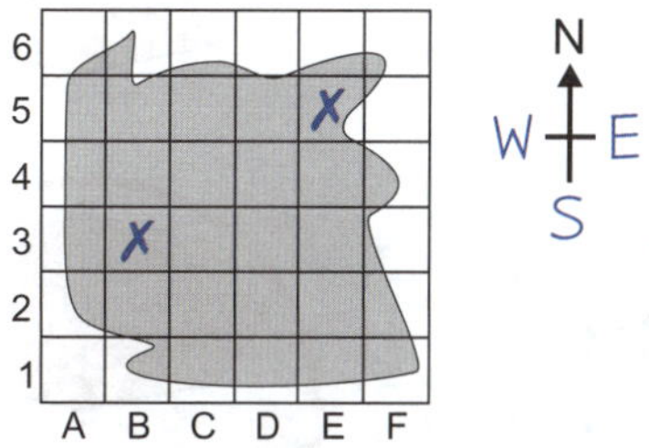

3 squares east then 2 squares north
OR 2 squares north then 3 squares east.

Make sure you know the four compass directions...

Coordinates are great for describing where something is on a grid. Just read down to the letter at the bottom and across to the number on the left. Then put the two together.

Symmetry

Polygons Can be Symmetrical

This shape has a mirror line. It is also called the line of symmetry.

Bob puts a mirror along the line of symmetry. It looks as if he can see the rest of the shape in the mirror.

Symmetrical shapes are exactly the same on both sides of the mirror line.

EXAMPLE: Complete the shape on the grid below to make it symmetrical.

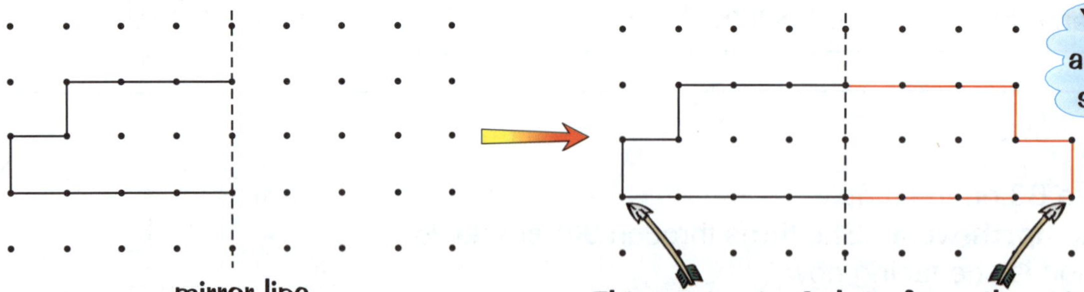

You can check your answer by tracing the shape and folding it.

This vertex is 4 dots from the mirror line. So put another vertex 4 dots away on the other side of the mirror line.

There Can be More Than One Line of Symmetry

EXAMPLE: Which of the shapes below have two or more lines of symmetry?

All regular polygons have lines of symmetry.

Some irregular polygons do too.

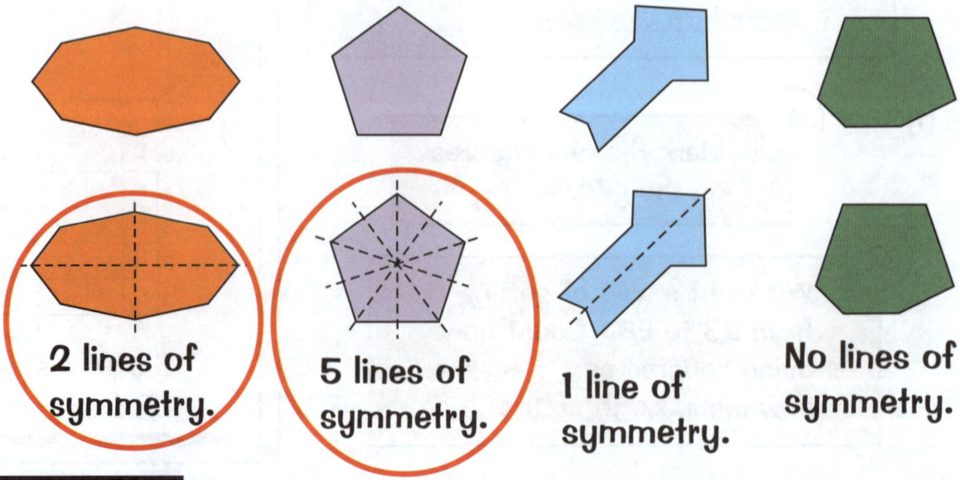

Learning Objective:

"I can work out how many lines of symmetry 2-D shapes have."

Symmetry

Question 1

Draw lines to complete the shape so that it is symmetrical in the mirror line.

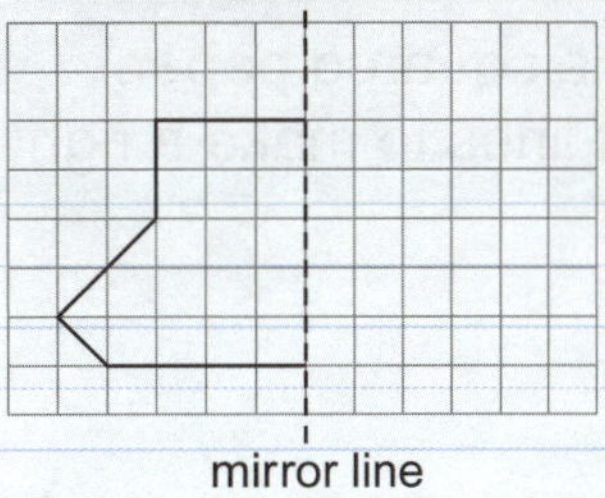

1. Count how many squares each vertex is from the mirror line.
2. Count the same number of squares on the other side of the mirror line and mark it with a cross.
3. Join the crosses together.

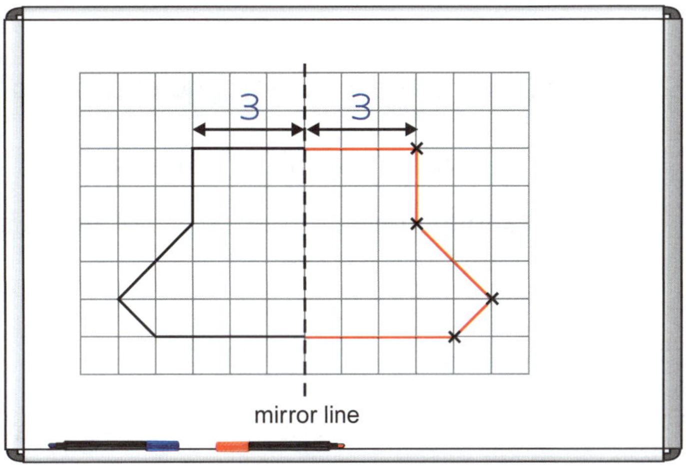

Question 2

Jade draws a shape with two lines of symmetry. Draw in the mirror lines.

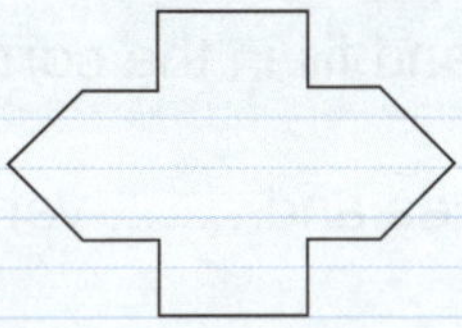

1. Look for the first mirror line. You could check by tracing the shape and folding the paper.
2. Then look for the second mirror line.
3. The question says that there are two lines of symmetry, so that's it.

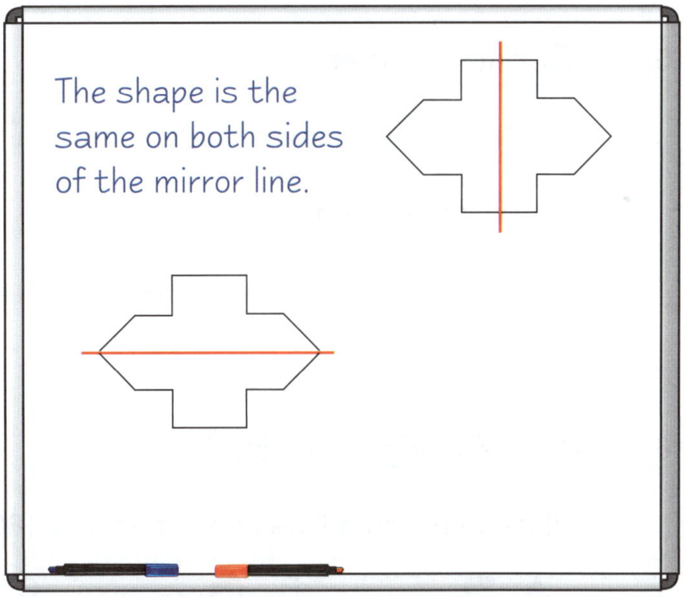

Symmetrical shapes are the same on both sides...

Shapes often have more than one line of symmetry. So don't stop looking after you've found one. Tracing the shape and folding the paper is useful for spotting mirror lines.

Practice Questions

1 Copy the grid onto some squared paper.
Draw two more straight lines to make a right-angled triangle.

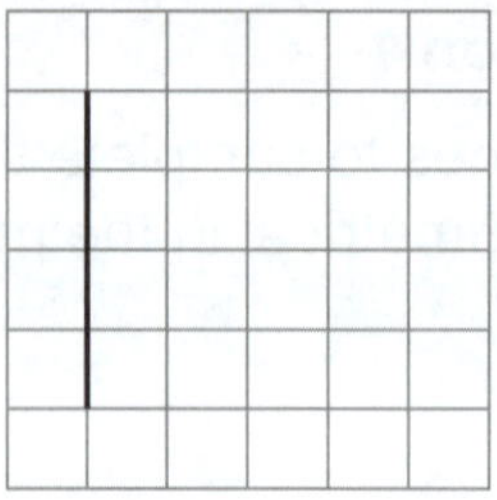

2 Copy the sentence below and choose from these words to fill in the gaps.

two **four** **one pair** **two pairs**

Rectangles have .... of equal sides and .... right angles.

3 Tanya drew this net for a cube.

Draw another cube net that she could have drawn.

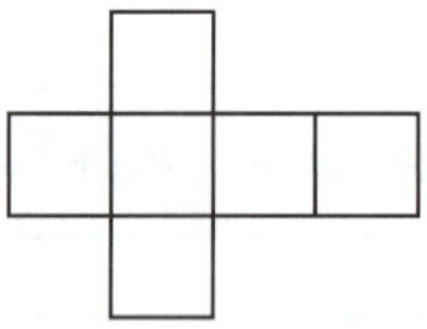

4 Copy this sentence and fill in the correct numbers in the gaps.

A cube has .... faces and .... vertices.

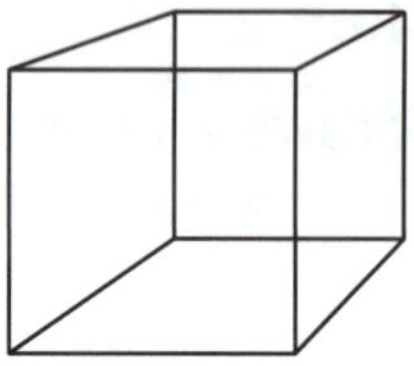

5 Look at the angles.

a) Which is the biggest angle?

b) Which is a right angle?

c) How many angles are larger than a right angle?

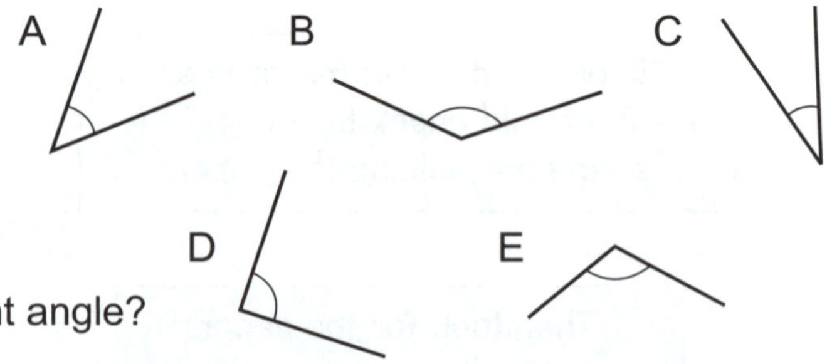

6 Dave is facing to the right.

Which direction will he face if he turns 180°?

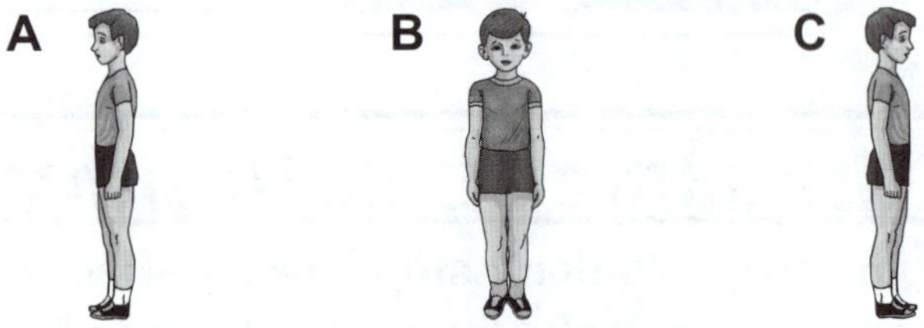

Practice Questions

7 Jack is playing a game. His counter is in square D6.

He moves it **3 squares down** and **2 squares left**.
Give the coordinates of the counter's new position.

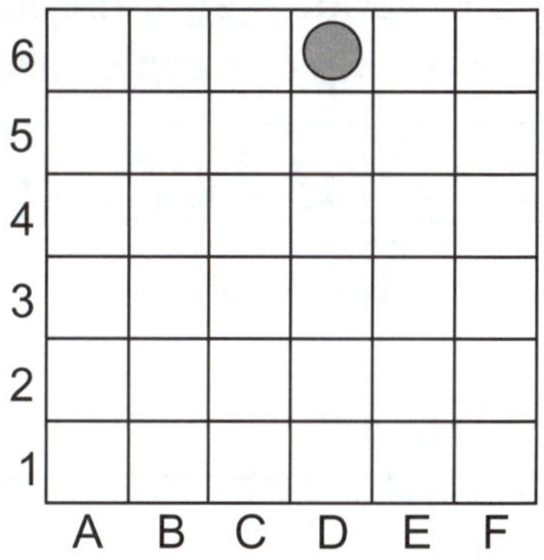

8 Helen is exploring an island. She walks from square B5 to square F1 on the map.

Describe her movement using compass directions.

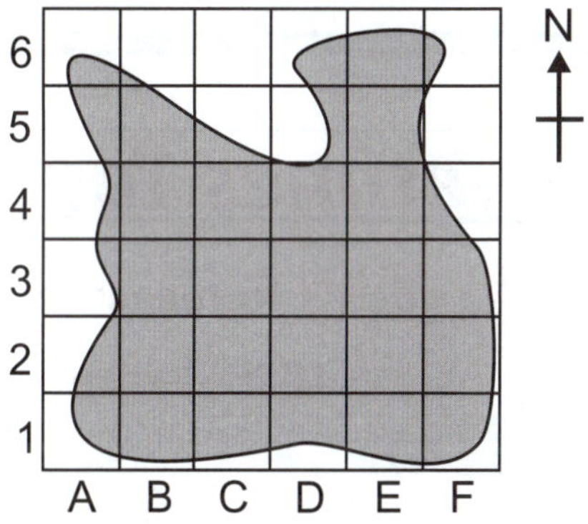

9 Which of these shapes have more than one line of symmetry?

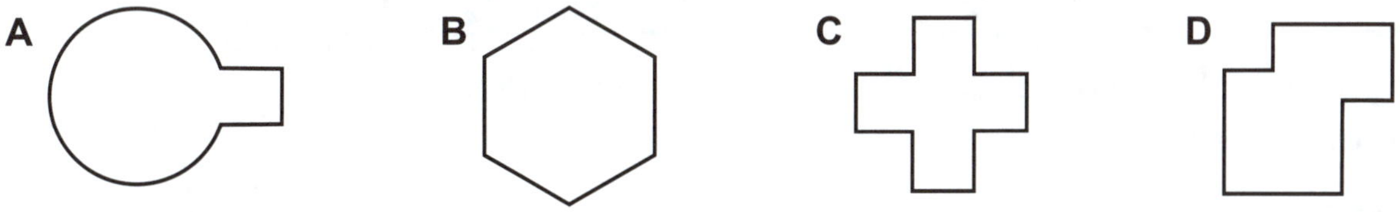

10 Copy the grids below.

Draw lines to complete the shapes so that they are symmetrical in the mirror line.

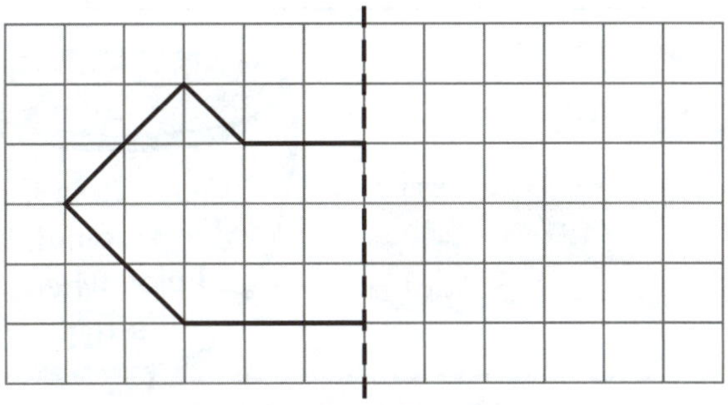

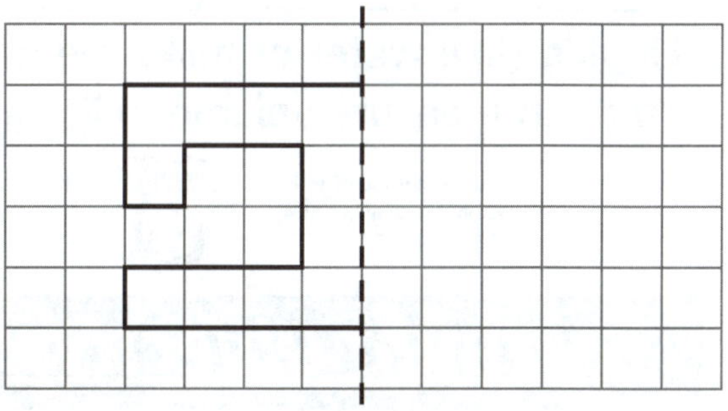

Units and Measures

This page is about metric units. These are the modern units that are most common these days. For example, people use metres instead of yards, and centimetres instead of inches.

There are Lots of Different Distance Units

You need to know about these 4 distance units.

millimetres (mm)
centimetres (cm) metres (m)
kilometres (km)

You can change from one unit into another.

10 mm = 1 cm
100 cm = 1 m
1000 m = 1 km

For example, my height is 1 m 64 cm. This is the same as 100 cm + 64 cm = 164 cm.

Sometimes You Have to Pick a Unit

Use big units to measure big distances. Use small units to measure small distances.

Unit → mm, cm, m, km

What you could measure → the width of your thumb, the length of a pencil, the height of a house, the distance across a country

Use a Balance or Scales to Find Mass

A balance or scales can tell you the mass of something.
Mass is measured in kilograms (kg) or grams (g).

1000 g = 1 kg

The mass of a sheet of A4 paper is about 5 grams.

Small cars have a mass of about 1000 kg.

Sugar often comes in 1 kg bags.

Volume is the Space Something Takes Up

Liquids (like water or milk) are measured by volume.
You can measure volume in litres (l) or millilitres (ml).

Large cartons of fruit juice are usually 1 litre.

1 l = 1000 ml

Learning Objective:

"I can choose suitable units to estimate and measure length."

Units and Measures

Question 1

Andy drives 6 km in his truck.
How many **metres** is this?

1. Write down how many metres there are in 1 km.
2. Multiply this by the total number of km that Andy drives.

1 km = 1000 m

Andy drives 6 km in total.
So in metres, this is:

6 km = 6 × 1000 m = 6000 m

Question 2

Say whether each sentence is likely to be true or not true.

A Lisa's car is 4 metres long.
B The mass of a camel is 100 g.
C A drink can contains 330 ml of lemonade.
D A mug is 14 mm tall.

A. Think of something you know the approximate length of in metres. Now compare that thing to a car.

B. Compare the camel's mass to something you know, like a 1 kg bag of sugar. Remember, 1 kg = 1000 g.

C. Think of something you know the capacity of, like a large juice carton. That's 1 litre, which is 1000 ml.

D. This one's easier. You can see how long 14 mm is on your ruler.

A door is about 2 metres high.
4 metres sounds OK for a car's length.
Sentence A is likely to be true.

A camel is much heavier than a bag of sugar. So 100 g is far too small.
Sentence B is not likely to be true.

Drink cans are smaller than large juice cartons. So 330 ml is about right.
Sentence C is likely to be true.

14 mm is between 1 cm and 2 cm.
It's far too short for a mug.
Sentence D is not likely to be true.

Learn the length, mass and volume of a few things...

Make sure you can say whether a unit is sensible for measuring something in. It'd just be plain daft to measure the distance between towns in mm, or the mass of a feather in kg.

Reading Scales

You Measure by Reading a Scale

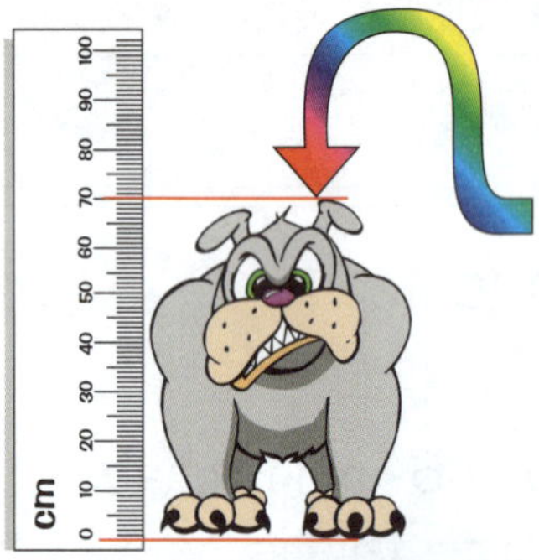

EXAMPLE: How tall is Dolly?

1) Draw a horizontal line from the top of her head to the ruler.
2) This line is at the 70 cm mark on the scale. So Dolly is 70 cm tall.

EXAMPLE: What is Bessie's mass?

The arrow points to a mark with no number. There are 4 marks between 450 g and 500 g. This makes 5 small divisions.

You have to work out what each small division is worth.

1) Find the difference between two numbered marks. → 500 g – 450 g = 50 g
2) Divide this difference by the number of small divisions. → 50 g ÷ 5 = 10 g

So each small division is worth 10 g.

ANSWER: Bessie's mass = 450 + 2 divisions = 450 + 20 = 470 g

You can Also Mark Answers on a Scale

EXAMPLE: Sid's mass is 1.5 kg. Draw an arrow on the scale to show this.

Find what 1 division is worth.

1) The difference between 2 kg and 1 kg is 2 – 1 = 1 kg.
2) There are 2 divisions between 1 and 2 on the scale. So 1 division is 1 kg ÷ 2 = 0.5 kg.

1.5 kg is the same as 1 kg + 0.5 kg
So your arrow must point to 1 kg + 1 division on the scale.

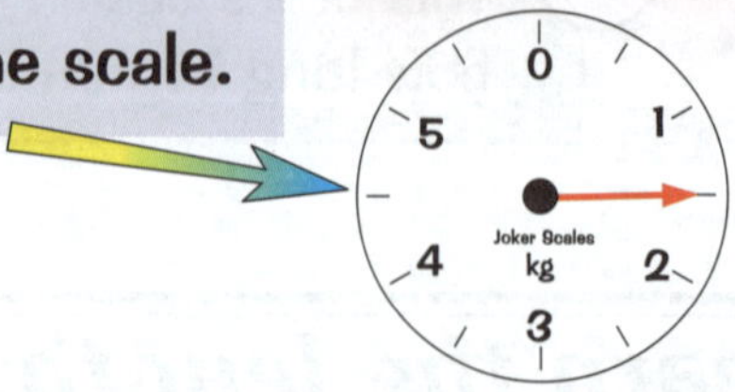

Learning Objective:

"I can say what one division on a scale is worth.
I can read a scale to the nearest division."

Reading Scales

Question 1

Karen is making a giant fruit pie. The recipe says she needs 5 kg of fruit.

a) What mass of fruit has she weighed out so far?
b) How much more fruit does she need to add, in kilograms?

a)

1. Work out what each small division on the scale is worth.

2. Add the whole kilograms to the number of small divisions.

b) Subtract the mass of fruit she has already from the total she needs.

There are 2 divisions between 3 kg and 4 kg on the scale.
So 1 division is: 1 kg ÷ 2 = 0.5 kg

The mass of the fruit is:
3 kg + 1 small division = 3 + 0.5 = 3.5 kg.

Karen has 3.5 kg. She needs 5 kg.
5 – 3.5 = 1.5
So she needs another 1.5 kg.

Question 2

This jug has water in it. Paul pours away 250 ml of the water.
Draw a line on the jug to show how much water will be left.

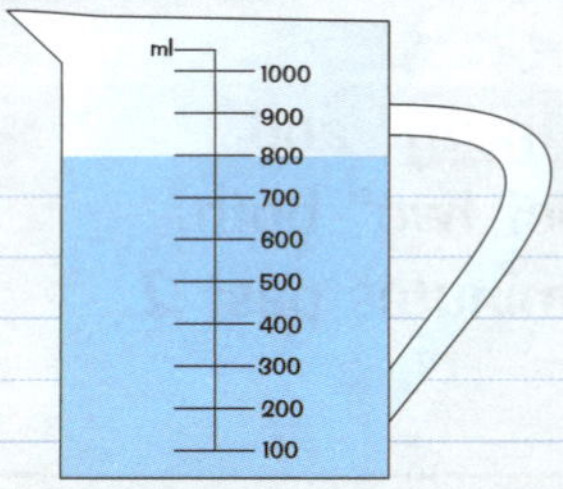

1. Read the scale to find out how much water is in the jug to start with.

2. Subtract the volume of water poured away from the volume there was to start with.

3. 550 is halfway between 500 and 600 ml, so draw a line halfway between the two marks.

The jug has 800 ml of water in it at first.

800 ml – 250 ml = 550 ml

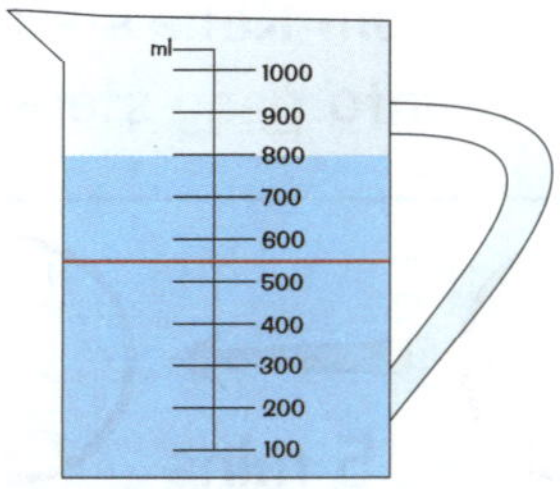

Counting the divisions is really important...

You might have to work out what each little division on a scale is worth. Don't panic...
Find the difference between two numbered marks then divide by the number of divisions.

Time

Analogue Clocks are the Ones with Hands

The little hand tells you about the hour and the big hand tells you about the minutes.

5 minutes past 12 | 10 minutes past 12 | 15 minutes past 12

Each time the big hand goes from one number to the next, another 5 minutes has passed.

After thirty minutes you start saying "minutes to" because it's closer to the next hour.

So you'd say 25 minutes to 3 instead of 35 minutes past 2.

15 minutes past = "quarter past"
30 minutes past = "half past"
15 minutes to = "quarter to"

Digital Clocks just have Numbers

Digital clocks are easy to read. You just say one number after the other.

EXAMPLE: This clock shows two-thirty. This number is the hour...

"Two-thirty" and "half past two" both mean 30 minutes past 2.

...and this is how many minutes past the hour.

You Can Work Out How Long Things Take

EXAMPLE: Katie leaves home at  and gets to school at 

How long does it take her to get to school?

Count on from Katie's start time to her finish time.
Split it up into easy steps. Count on to a full hour or half-hour first:

 + 5 mins  + 30 mins  + 5 mins 

So it takes her 5 + 30 + 5 = 40 minutes.

Learning Objective:

"I can tell the time to the nearest 5 minutes.
I can work out how long an activity takes."

Time

Question 1

Mark leaves for school at  He arrives at school at 

How long does his journey take?

1. Split the journey time up into easy steps.

2. Add the times of the easy steps together.

In easy steps:

= 5 minutes

= 30 minutes

= 10 minutes

5 + 30 + 10 = 45 minutes

Question 2

A cake is put in the oven at 10:30. It takes 55 minutes to cook.

What time will the cake be ready?

1. Divide the time into smaller steps. It's 30 minutes to the next hour, so have "30 minutes" as one of your steps.

2. Add each step onto the starting time.

OR You could also add an hour (60 minutes) then subtract 5 minutes.

55 minutes = 30 mins + 25 mins

10.30 + 30 minutes = 11.00
11.00 + 25 minutes = 11.25
The cake will be ready at 11.25.

OR
55 minutes = 1 hour – 5 minutes
10.30 + 1 hour = 11.30
11.30 – 5 minutes = 11.25

Clocks with hands, watches with feet...

Always remember that an hour is 60 minutes, not 100 (loads of people make that mistake). When you're solving time problems, it's usually easiest to split them up into easy steps.

Practice Questions

1 Match each of these measurements to an equivalent length in one of the boxes.

2 m   2 cm   2000 mm   2 km

2000 m	200 cm	20 mm	2 m

2 Convert the following measurements:

a) 400 cm into metres

b) 3500 m into kilometres

c) 7000 g into kilograms

d) 2 l into millilitres

3 John and June have a competition to see who can grow the taller sunflower. John's sunflower grows to 1 metre and 45 centimetres. June's is 152 centimetres.

Whose sunflower is taller?

4 Jenny is 2 kilometres away from the nearest shop. Katherine is 2200 m away from the same shop.

Who is nearer the shop?

5 Asif has $4\frac{1}{2}$ l of custard. He wants to pour it into buckets. Each bucket can hold 1000 ml of custard.

How many buckets will Asif need to hold all the custard?

6 Calum wants to measure the height of his pet chicken.

How tall is the chicken in centimetres?

Practice Questions

7 What is the mass of this cake in grams?

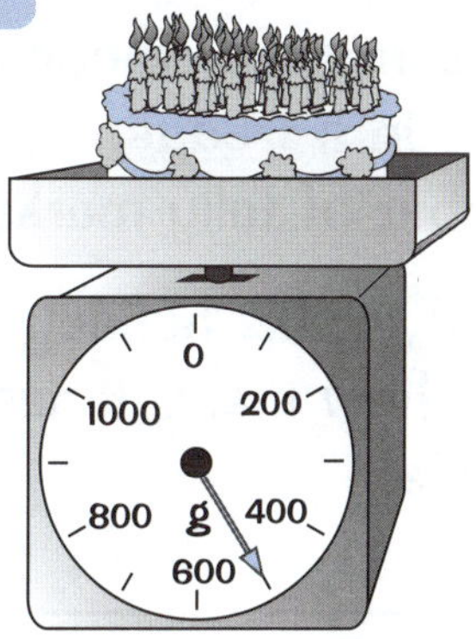

8 Kerry has four books. Each book has the same mass.

She weighs two of the books.

a) What is the total mass of the books on the scales, in kilograms?

b) What is the mass of one book in kg?

c) What would the mass of all four of Kerry's books be in kg?

9 Draw an analogue clock face like the one on the right.

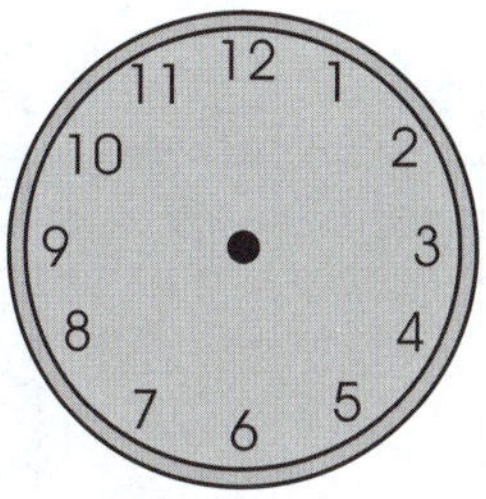

a) Draw on the hands to show the time 3 o'clock.

b) What will the time be one hour later?

c) Draw a new clock.
Draw the position of the hands 50 minutes after your answer to b).

10 Tom is on the train from London to Manchester.

The train leaves London at 8:30. It arrives in Manchester at 11:20.

How long does Tom's journey take?

Tables and Charts

These are tally marks. They help you keep count.

Tally marks aren't very easy to read, though. It's easier to show numbers in a frequency table. You just count up the number of tally marks.

Bert went to Monster World for his holidays. This frequency table shows how many times he went on the Monster Ride.

	Tally	Frequency
Monday	ǀǀ	2
Tuesday	卌	5
Wednesday	卌 ǀǀǀ	8
Thursday	ǀǀǀ	3
Friday	ǀǀ	2

Tally marks are always grouped in fives.

Pictograms are Numbers in Pictures

Pictograms use pictures to show how many times something happens.

For example:

= 2 goes on the Monster Ride

This is the key. It tells you what one picture on the pictogram represents.

Bert had three goes on the Monster Ride on Thursday.

Bar Charts Show Things at a Glance

Bar charts make it easy to compare things.

Bar charts can also be called block graphs.

The height of each bar shows how many times Bert went on the ride.

Just read across from the top of the bar to the number on the left.

Bar charts have two axes. This is the horizontal axis. The other is the vertical axis.

Learning Objective:

"I can show information in a bar chart or pictogram."

Tables and Charts

Question 1

Sam asked people in his class what their favourite colour was.

a) What colour did the **third highest** number of people choose?

b) How many more people said **red** than said **yellow**?

Colour	Number of people
blue	7
green	3
purple	4
red	6
yellow	2

a) **1** Find the third highest number in the "Number of people" column.

2 Read off the colour.

b) **1** Find how many people chose red and how many chose yellow.

2 Find the difference between them.

a) The third highest number of people is 4.

4 people chose purple.

b) 6 people chose red.
2 people chose yellow.

6 – 2 = 4 more people said red than said yellow.

Question 2

A shop recorded the number of rain hats it sold over a bank holiday weekend.

They sold **5** hats on **Saturday**, **7** hats on **Sunday** and **8** hats on **Monday**.

Complete this pictogram to show the data.

Saturday	
Sunday	
Monday	

= 2 hats   = 1 hat

1 Read the key. If one full symbol stands for 2 hats sold, then...

2 ...5 hats sold is 2½ symbols.
7 hats sold is 3½ symbols.
8 hats sold is 4 symbols.

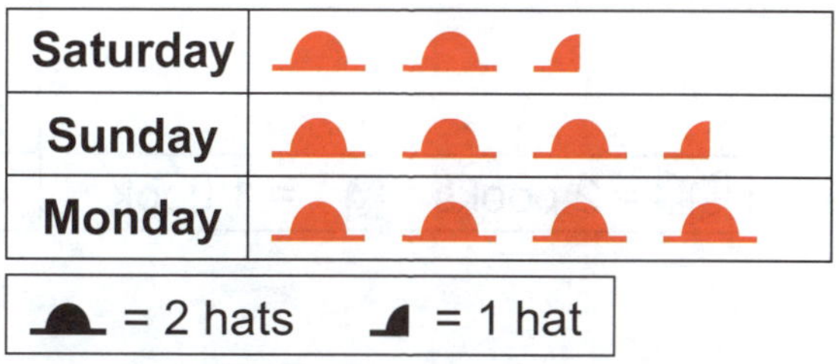

Graphs make it easier to compare things...

Pictograms and bar charts let you see at a glance how big one number is compared to another. That's harder to do from a list of numbers in a table.

Practice Questions

1 Steven counted the number of cars of different colours in a car park.

Write the numbers that should go in the frequency column.

Colour	Tally	Frequency
black	III	
blue	𝍸	
red	𝍸 I	
silver	𝍸 II	
white	I	

2 A group of children have been out collecting conkers. The chart shows how many conkers each child has.

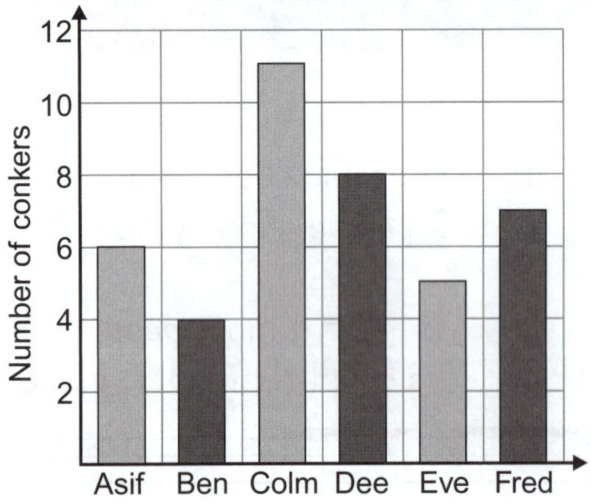

a) How many conkers does Eve have?

b) How many more conkers does Colm have than Ben?

3 The table shows the number of books borrowed from a library each hour one afternoon.

Time	Number of books
12 – 1pm	6
1 – 2pm	9
2 – 3pm	7
3 – 4pm	3
4 – 5pm	8

Copy and complete this pictogram showing the information.

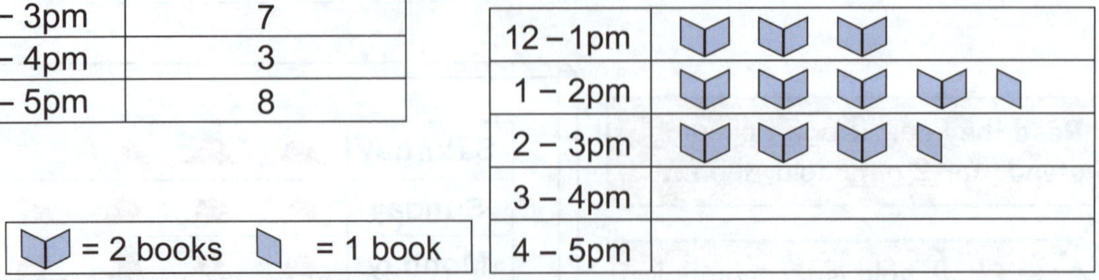

4 The pictogram shows the number of goals scored by two football teams in a season.

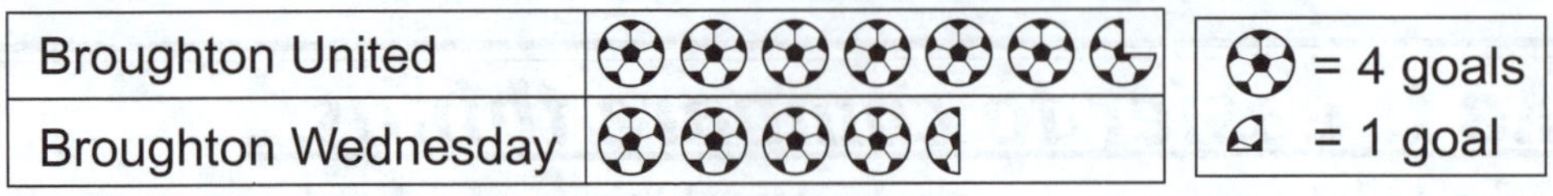

How many goals did each team score?

Practice Questions

5 Jasmine recorded the shoe size of each child in her class.

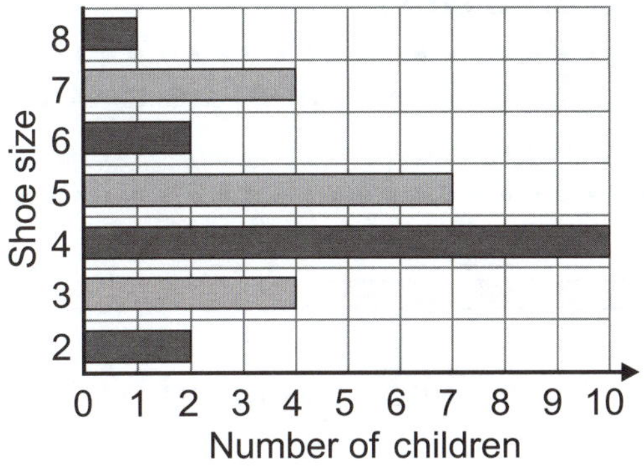

a) How many children wore size 4 shoes?

b) How many children wore shoes that were size 5 or bigger?

6 Yvonne collects marbles.
She sorted her marbles by colour and drew a pictogram.

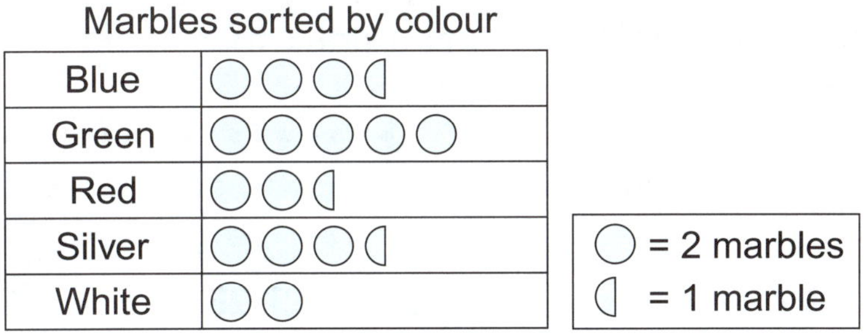

a) How many white marbles does Yvonne have?

b) After she made her pictogram, Yvonne found a small bag of marbles she had missed.
It contained 3 blue marbles, 1 green marble and 2 red marbles.
Copy the pictogram, then add these extra marbles to your copy.

7 Matthew asked the children in his class what their favourite fruit was.
He recorded his results in a frequency table.

Fruit	Number of children
apple	6
banana	8
orange	5
grapes	7
pear	2

Copy and complete the bar chart showing the information.

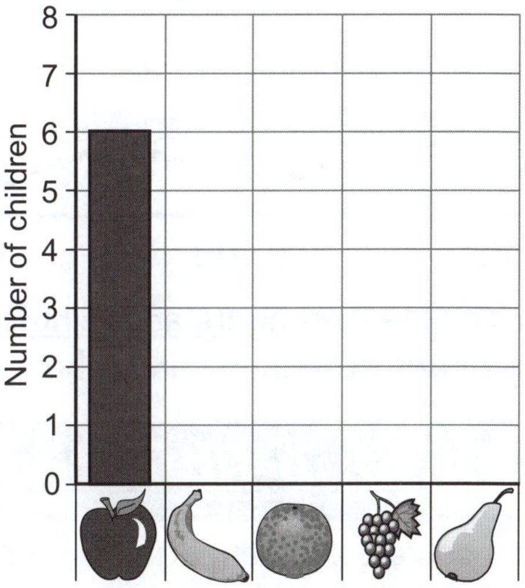

Problem Solving

Some Problems Just Need One Step

You just need to do one calculation to solve some problems.

EXAMPLE: Emma needs 4 pieces of ribbon. Each piece must be 8 cm long. What total length of ribbon should she buy?

You need to work out what 4 lots of 8 are. This is multiplication.

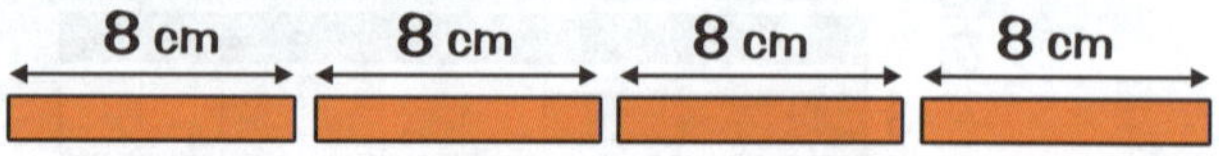

$$4 \times 8 = 32$$

The ribbon needs to be 32 cm long.

Other Problems Need More Than One Step

You need to do more than one calculation to solve some problems.

EXAMPLE: Richard buys a lolly that costs 85p and a drink that costs 40p. How much change does he get from £5?

First, find out how much Richard spends in total.

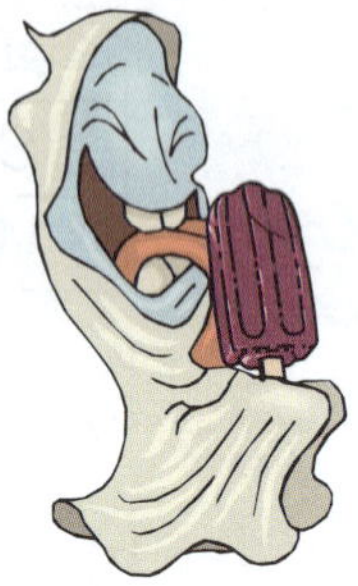

$$85 + 40 = 125$$

So Richard spends 125p or £1.25

Then find out how much change he gets.

$$£5 - £1.25 = £3.75$$

So Richard gets £3.75 change.

Some Problems Involve Time

EXAMPLE: Jason got on the bus at 9:20. He got off again at 10:40. How long was the bus ride in hours and minutes?

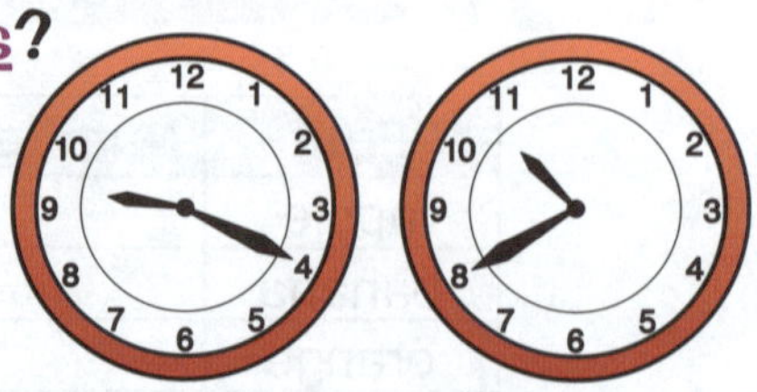

Break up the time into simple steps.

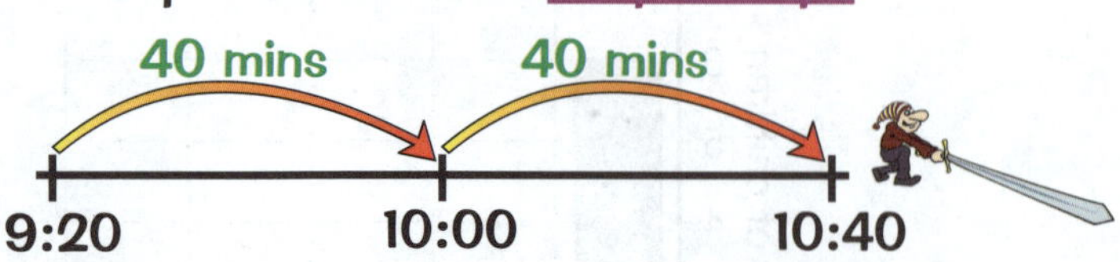

40 mins + 40 mins = 80 minutes

Now change it to hours and minutes. There are 60 minutes in an hour.

80 minutes = 60 minutes + 20 minutes
= 1 hour + 20 minutes

So the journey took 1 hour and 20 minutes.

Learning Objective:

"I can solve a problem by choosing the calculation I should do."

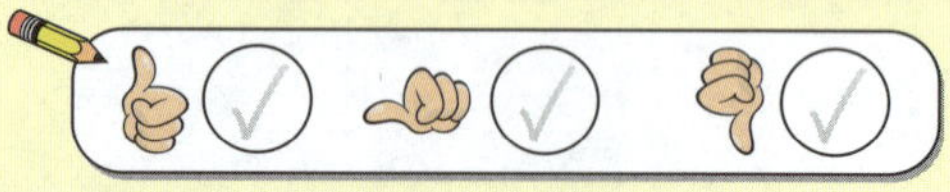

Problem Solving

Question 1

Andrew and Tina are having a party. They buy a packet of balloons for 96p. They share the cost of the balloons equally. How much do they each pay?

1. Andrew and Tina split the cost of the balloons equally. So you need to find half of 96p or 96p ÷ 2.
2. It's easier to find half of 96p if you partition it. Then find half of each bit. You can partition 96 into 90 + 6, but 90 is tricky to halve. So use 80 + 10 + 6.
3. Then add up all the halves to find the amount they each paid.

They each spent 96p ÷ 2

96p = 80p + 10p + 6p

half ↓ half ↓ half ↓

40p + 5p + 3p

40p + 5p + 3p = 48p

They each paid 48p

Question 2

Mohammed starts eating his dinner at 4:50. It takes him 20 minutes to eat it. He goes to bed at 8:15. Once he has finished dinner, how long is it before he goes to bed? Give your answer in hours and minutes.

1. First work out what time Mohammed finishes his dinner. Make a time line and count on 20 minutes from 4:50.
2. Now find out how long it is until he goes to bed. Make a time line that goes from 5:10 to 8:15 and count along it in simple steps.
3. Now add up the minutes and hours.
4. 65 minutes is more than 1 hour. Change it to hours and minutes to get the final answer.

Mohammed finishes dinner at 5:10.

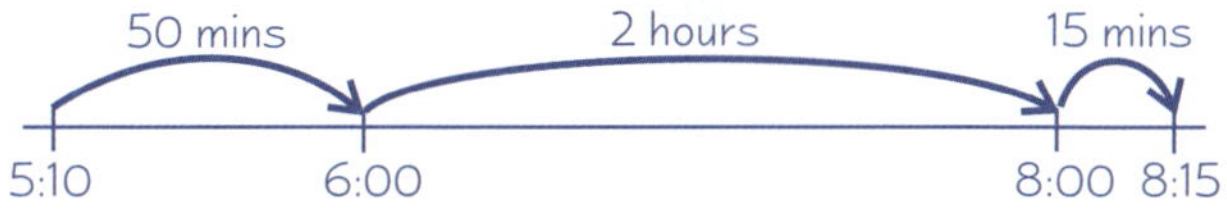

50 mins + 2 hours + 15 mins

= 2 hours and 65 minutes

= 2 hours + 1 hour + 5 mins

= 3 hours and 5 mins

Read the problem twice before you start...

Make sure you understand what the problem is asking you to find before you start adding numbers willy-nilly. And check your answer makes sense by reading the question again.

Practice Questions

1 Ellen is making a paper chain. It has to be 300 cm long.
She has made 140 cm so far.

How many more centimetres must she make?

2 This table shows how many kilometres Sarah cycled each day for three days.

Day	Friday	Saturday	Sunday
Distance (km)	38	76	50

a) How many kilometres did she cycle altogether?

b) On Saturday she started cycling at 8:30am. She finished at 10:15am.
How long did she cycle for in hours and minutes?

3 James has 38 sweets. He wants to share them all out equally between his four friends.

Will there be any sweets left over? If so, how many?

4 Sharon is a cleaner. She works on five days each week.
Each day she works for four hours.

a) She gets paid £6 per hour. How much does she get paid a week?

b) Sharon's sister is a cleaner too.
She works on three days each week and she works for 8 hours each day.
How many more hours does she work than Sharon?

5 Dave has a bag of 500 rubber bands. He flicks 320 of them at Molly.
Molly flicks 60 back. Dave catches them and puts them back in the bag.

How many rubber bands are in Dave's bag now?

6 Peter gets in the bath at 6:20. He spends 45 minutes in the bath.

At what time does he get out of the bath?

Practice Questions

7 These clocks show the time that Ruby woke up one morning and the time she fell asleep that night.

a) How long was Ruby awake that day?
Give your answer in hours and minutes.

b) Ruby spent 6 hours 30 minutes at school that day.
How long was she awake but not at school?
Give your answer in hours and minutes.

Ruby woke up at:

Ruby went to sleep up at:

8 There are 718 children at Greenodd Primary School.
One day 552 children wear boots, 110 wear trainers and the rest wear sandals.

How many children wore sandals?

9 Joe has 235 points in a game. Hannah has twice as many.

How many points does Hannah have?

10 Here are some prices for rides at the fair.

a) Rosie goes on the log flume twice and the dodgems once.
How much does she spend?

b) On Monday mornings all rides are half price.
How much would Rosie have saved if she had gone to the fair on a Monday morning?

11 Carl and Laura are saving up together to buy a computer game costing £11.99
Carl has saved up £4.50 and Laura has saved up £2.20

How much more money must they save up to buy the computer game?

12 Jane buys 500 g of flour. She uses half of it to make a cake and 185 g to make pancakes.

How many grams of flour does she have left?

Answers

Pages 14-15 — Section One

1) 84, 109, 227, 284, 643

2) The dial is really just a curved number line. The temperature goes down 6 °C, so move 6 places left.
–4 °C
For help with questions like this, look at the NUMBERS AND NUMBER LINES pages.

3) a) 5 **>** 1
b) 8.4 **<** 9.4
c) –8 **<** 7

4) 13.45 = 1 ten + 3 units + 4 tenths + 5 hundredths = **10** + **3** + **0.4** + **0.05**

5) a) and b)
Each unit is divided into tenths.
1.2 is 1 unit + 2 tenths along.
The hundredths aren't marked, but 1.85 is half way between 1.8 and 1.9.

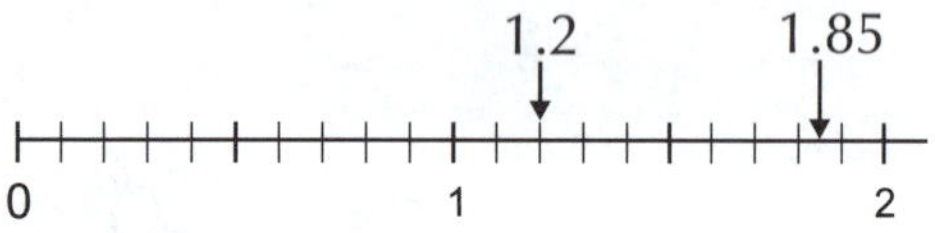

Look at the DECIMALS pages for more help.

6) 5 cm = 5 hundredths of a metre = 5 × 0.01 m = 0.05 m.
1 + 0.05 = **1.05 m**

7) a) There are 3 days, so Carlos eats $\frac{1}{3}$ of the tomatoes on each day.
$\frac{1}{3}$ of 9 = 9 ÷ 3 = **3**

b) Carlos eats $\frac{1}{3}$ of the pie each day.
On Friday and Saturday he eats
$\frac{1}{3} \times 2 = \mathbf{\frac{2}{3}}$ in total.

8) a) **B** and **D** (They both have 9 out of 16 squares shaded.)

b) $\frac{9}{16}$

9) To get from 3 hours of banjo practice to 6, you multiply by 2. So do the same to the hours of TV.
So she can watch TV for 2 × 1 hour
= **2 hours**

10) To get from 6 to 12 you multiply by 2.
So multiply the 1 by 2 as well.
1 × 2 = **2 red apples**

11) Round each number to the nearest 10.
a) 20 + 90 = 110
b) 90 – 20 = 70
If you find this tricky, look at the ROUNDING pages.

Pages 22-23 — Section Two

1) 200 m + 600 m + 300 m

2) 11 – 7 = 4, so 110 – 70 = 40
5 – 1 = 4, so 50 – 10 = 40
17 – 13 = 4, so 170 – 130 = 40

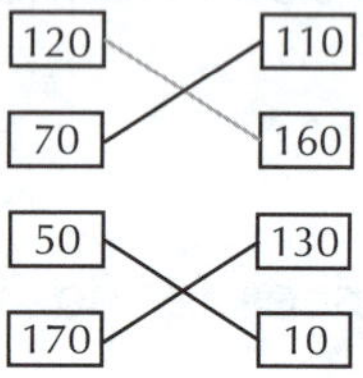

3) Make each number 10 times smaller to make an easier calculation.
15 – 6 – 3 = 6
Make the numbers 10 times bigger again.
150 – 60 – 30 = **60**

4) You need to work out 50 + 80 – 70.
Do 5 + 8 – 7, then multiply by 10.
5 + 8 = 13. 13 – 7 = 6.
6 × 10 = 60.
So Jenny has **60 points** altogether.

5) 100 – 79 = 21 or 100 – 21 = 79

6) a) 77 – 42 = 35. So Tasha is **right**.
b) 8 × 4 = 32. So Tasha is **wrong**.
c) 45 + 36 = 81. So Tasha is **right**.
Doing the inverse calculation is one good way to check your answer. For more help, have a look at the CHECKING CALCULATIONS pages.

Answers

7) a) 100 – 35 = 65
So 35 + **65** = 100
b) 48 ÷ 8 = 6
So 8 × **6** = 48
c) 9 × 4 = 36
So **36** ÷ 4 = 9

8) The same number should be in both boxes.
E.g. 58 + **62** – **62** = 58

9) 122 – 43 rounds to 120 – 40. 120 – 40 = 80.
Anna's answer is much smaller than 80, so she is likely to be **wrong**.

10) Round 23 down to 20.
20 × 5 = **100 parcels**.
Rounding is a good way to quickly estimate the answer to a calculation. If you want to know more, check out the CHECKING CALCULATIONS pages.

11) 6 × 9 = **54**

12) 6 × 4 = 24 puppies
So altogether there are 24 + 4 = **28 dogs**.

13) There are 6 people (Dave + 5 friends) sharing the 42 chocolates.
Use the 6 times table.
5 × 6 = 30
6 × 6 = 36
7 × 6 = 42
So 42 ÷ 6 = 7
Each person gets **7** chocolates.

14)a) 8 × 5p = **40p**
b) Yes, it ends in a 0.

15) 32, 38, 44, 42, 30, 34, 36, 28
(Multiples of 2 are just even numbers.)

16) E.g. **9**, **10** and **11** (9 + 10 + 11 = 30)

Pages 32-33 — Section Three

1) 82 – 35 = 82 – 30 – 5 = 52 – 5 = **47**

2) 32 – 15 = 32 – 10 – 5 = 22 – 5 = **17**

3) 37 + 12 = 37 + 10 + 2 = 47 + 2
= **49** years old

4) Change both amounts to pence.

```
  325
+ 144
+   9
+  60
+ 400
  469
```

So he spends **£4.69**

5)

```
  289
+ 145
+  14
+ 120
+ 300
  434
```

He spends **£434**.

6) 187 = 100 + 80 + 7. So 224 – 187 =

```
  224
-   7
  217
-  80
  137
- 100
   37
```

7) a) £1.05 = 105p

```
  105
+  65
+  10
+  60
+ 100
  170
```

170 = **£1.70**

b) £3.20 = 320p

```
  320
+  54
+   4
+  70
+ 300
  374
```

374 = **£3.74**

For help with additions like this, take a look at the WRITTEN ADDING AND SUBTRACTING pages.

8) 80 ÷ 5 = 50 ÷ 5 + 30 ÷ 5
= 10 + 6 = **16**

Answers

9) $46 \div 6 = 36 \div 6 + 10 \div 6$
$= 6 + 1\ r4 = 7\ r4$
There are **4** buns left over.

10)

×	4
50	200
5	20
	220p = **£2.20**

11)a) $4 \times 6 = 24$, so $4 \times 60 =$ **240**
b) $45 \div 3 = 30 \div 3 + 15 \div 3$
$= 10 + 5 =$ **15**

12) £3.75 – £1.34 = **£2.41**

13) 2 × 17.50 = £35
£35 + £10 = **£45**

14) 21

15) 192 ÷ 6 = 32.
So she must buy **32 packs**.

16) 46p × 3 = 138p
200p – 138p = **62p**
Calculators only make calculations easier if you know how to use them. If you need more help, check out the CALCULATORS pages.

17) 34.7 + 62.7 – 106.8 = **–9.4°**

Pages 44-45 — Section Four

1) E.g.

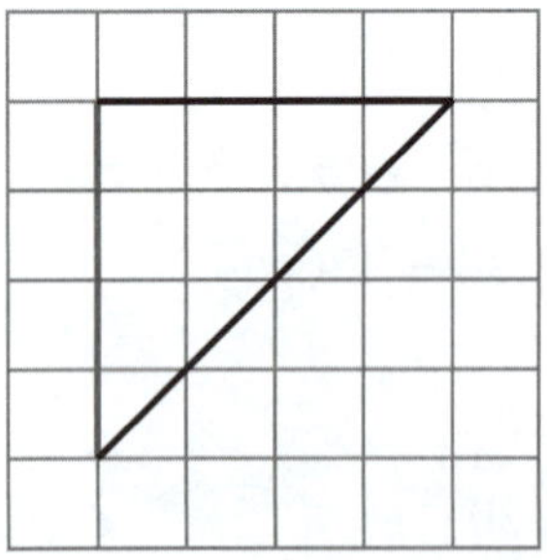

2) Rectangles have **two pairs** of equal sides and **four** right angles.

3) E.g.

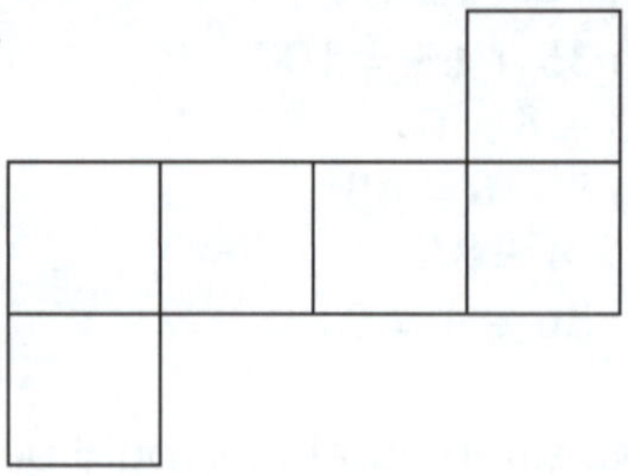

4) A cube has **6** faces and **8** vertices.

5) a) B
b) D
c) 2 (B and E)

6) A

7) B3

8) E.g.
She walks **4 squares south** and **4 squares east**. (Allow any answer that gets her from B5 to F1 without having to go in the water.)
For more help using compass directions, take a look at the COORDINATES pages.

9) Shapes **B** and **C**.

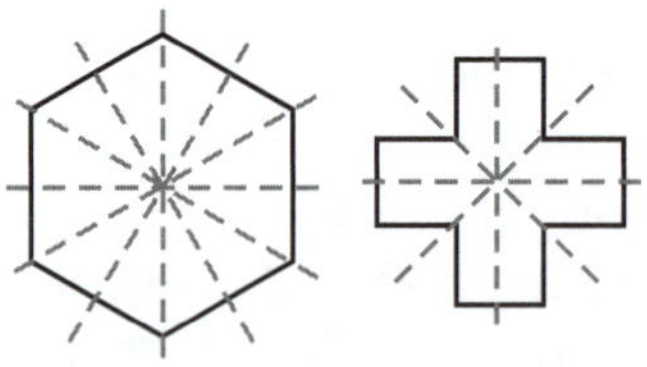

10)

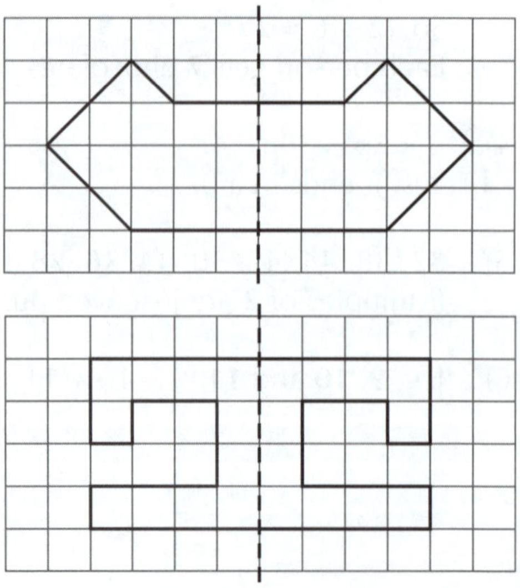

If you found this question difficult, check out the pages on SYMMETRY for more help.

Answers

Pages 52-53 — Section Five

1) 2 m = 200 cm
2 cm = 20 mm
2000 mm = 2 m
2 km = 2000 m

2) a) 100 cm in 1 m, so 400 cm = **4 metres**
b) 1000 m in 1 km, so 3500 m = **3.5 kilometres**
c) 1000 g = 1 kg, so 7000 g = **7 kilograms**
d) 1 l = 1000 ml, so 2 l = **2000 millilitres**

3) 152 cm = 1 m and 52 cm.
So, **June's** sunflower is taller.

4) 2 km = 2000 m.
So, **Jenny** is nearer the shop.
Make the units the same so you can compare measurements. The pages on UNITS AND MEASURES will help.

5) 1000 ml = 1 l. So **5 buckets** are needed to hold $4\frac{1}{2}$ litres.
(You can't have $4\frac{1}{2}$ buckets — you need one whole bucket to hold $\frac{1}{2}$ l of custard.)

6) 38 cm

7) 500 g
Always count the divisions and work out how much they're each worth. For more help see the pages on READING SCALES.

8) a) 1 kg
b) 1 kg ÷ 2 = $\frac{1}{2}$ **kg** or **0.5 kg**
c) 1 × 2 = **2 kg**

9) a)

b) 4 o'clock or 4:00

c)

10) 8:30 + 30 mins = 9:00
9:00 + 2 hours = 11:00
11:00 + 20 mins = 11:20
30 mins + 2 hours + 20 mins
= **2 hours 50 minutes**
If you found it difficult to work out how long Tom's journey took, have a look at the pages on TIME.

Pages 56-57 — Section Six

1)

Colour	Tally	Frequency
black	|||	3
blue	~~||||~~	5
red	~~||||~~ |	6
silver	~~||||~~ ||	7
white	|	1

2) a) 5
b) 11 – 4 = **7**

3)

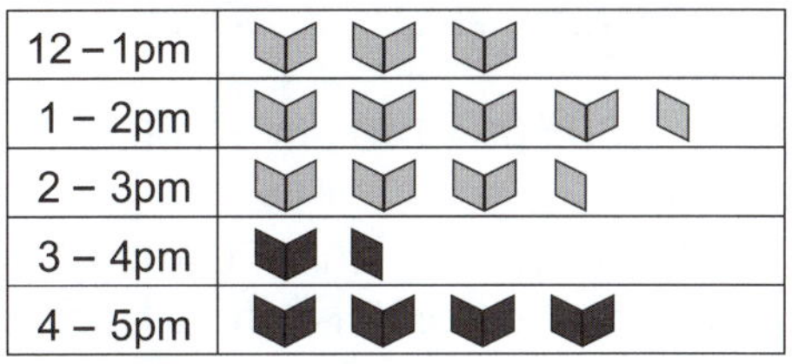

4) Broughton United: **27 goals**
Broughton Wednesday: **18 goals**
Remember to look at the key to work out what 1 symbol stands for. For more help on pictograms, see the TABLES AND CHARTS pages.

Answers

5) a) 10
b) size 5 = 7 children
size 6 = 2 children
size 7 = 4 children
size 8 = 1 child
So the number of children with size 5 or bigger shoes = 7 + 2 + 4 + 1 = **14**

6) a) 4 white marbles
b)
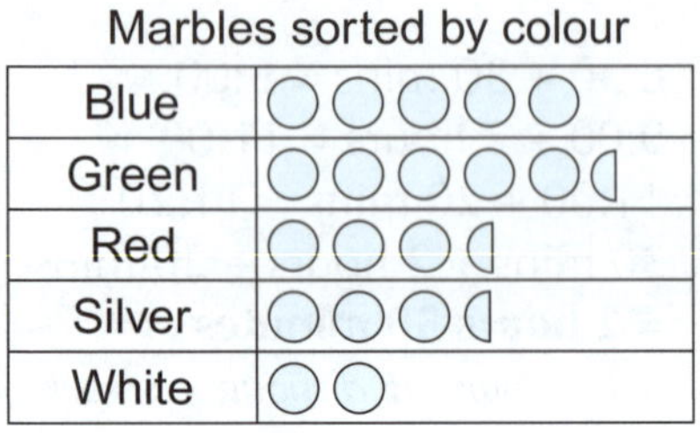

7)
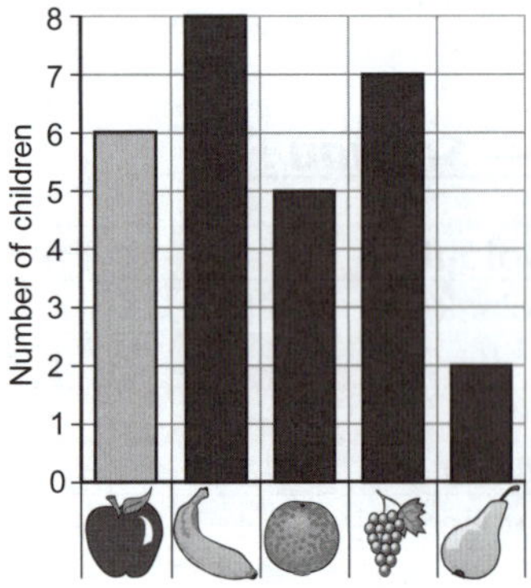

If you need help with bar charts, look at the pages on TABLES AND CHARTS.

Pages 60-61 — Section Seven

1) 300 cm – 140 cm = **160 cm**

2) a) 38 km + 76 km + 50 km = **164 km**
b) 8:30 to 10:00 is 1 hour and 30 minutes.
10:00 to 10:15 is 15 minutes
1 hour and 30 minutes + 15 minutes = **1 hour and 45 minutes**

3) 38 is not a multiple of 4.
The nearest multiple of 4 that's less than 38 is 36. (36 ÷ 4 = 9)
So there will be 38 – 36 = **2 sweets** left over.

4) a) 5 × 4 hours = 20 hours
£6 × 20 = **£120**
b) Her sister works 3 × 8 hours = 24 hours
24 hours – 20 hours = **4 hours**

5) 500 – 320 = 180
180 + 60 = **240**

6) Count on 45 minutes from 6:20 in easy steps:
6:20 to 7:00 is 40 minutes.
7:00 to 7:05 is 5 minutes.
So Peter gets out of the bath at **7:05**.

7) a) Ruby woke up at 7:25am
Ruby went to sleep at 9:35pm
7:25am to 7:25pm is 12 hours.
7:25pm to 9:25pm is 2 hours.
9:25 to 9:35 is 10 minutes.
So Ruby was awake for 12 hours + 2 hours + 10 minutes = **14 hr 10 min.**
b) You need to subtract 6 hr 30 min from 14 hr 10 min. Do it in easy steps:
14 hr 10 min – 6 hours = 8 hr 10 min,
8 hr 10 min – 10 min = 8 hr.
8 hr – 20 min = **7 hr 40 min**
If you're having problems with questions on time intervals, take a look at the pages on PROBLEM SOLVING and TIME.

8) 718 – 552 – 110 = **56**

9) 235 × 2 = **470**

10) a) 84p × 2 = 168p
168p + 66p = 234p = **£2.34**
b) £2.34 ÷ 2 = **£1.17**

11) £4.50 + £2.20 = £6.70
£11.99 – £6.70 = **£5.29**

12) 500 g ÷ 2 = 250 g
250 g + 185 g = 435 g
500 g – 435 g = **65 g**
This problem has three steps. If you need help with multistep problems check out the PROBLEM SOLVING pages.

Index

Index